Shifting For Himself

or, Gilbert Greyson's Fortunes

I0756424

Jr. Horatio Alger

Alpha Editions

This edition published in 2023

ISBN : 9789357942065

Design and Setting By
Alpha Editions
www.alphaedis.com
Email - info@alphaedis.com

Contents

PREFACE. - 1 -

CHAPTER I. TWO SCHOOL-FELLOWS. - 2 -

CHAPTER II. THE GUARDIAN'S LETTER - 7 -

CHAPTER III. RICHARD BRIGGS - 12 -

CHAPTER IV. GILBERT MAKES A NEW ACQUAINTANCE - 17 -

CHAPTER V. AT THE DINNER-TABLE - 22 -

CHAPTER VI. HOW GILBERT GOT ON. - 27 -

CHAPTER VII. A SPITEFUL WOMAN - 33 -

CHAPTER VIII. GILBERT GETS A PLACE. - 38 -

CHAPTER IX. THE FIRST DAY IN BUSINESS - 43 -

CHAPTER X. THE NEW BOARDING-HOUSE. - 48 -

CHAPTER XI. A NEW ARRANGEMENT. - 53 -

CHAPTER XII. RANDOLPH'S CALL. - 58 -

CHAPTER XIII. GILBERT CALLS ON THE VIVIANS - 63 -

CHAPTER XIV. A PLEASANT EVENING. - 68 -

CHAPTER XV. AT STEINWAY HALL. - 73 -

CHAPTER XVI. A PLOT AGAINST GILBERT. - 78 -

CHAPTER XVII. THE PLOT SUCCEEDS. - 83 -

CHAPTER XVIII. AN HUMBLE FRIEND. - 88 -

CHAPTER XIX. A DOMESTIC DISCUSSION. - 93 -

CHAPTER XX. A FEMALE FOE. - 96 -

CHAPTER XXI. ALPHONSO JONES. - 101 -

CHAPTER XXII. COUNT ERNEST DE MONTMORENCY. - 105 -

CHAPTER XXIII. THE LITTLE FLOWER-GIRL. - 108 -

CHAPTER XXIV. EMMA'S FATHER. - 112 -

CHAPTER XXV. GILBERT IN A TIGHT PLACE. - 116 -

CHAPTER XXVI. THE COUNT'S SECRET. - 119 -

CHAPTER XXVII. HARD UP. - 123 -

CHAPTER XXVIII. AN UNSATISFACTORY CALL. - 126 -

CHAPTER XXIX. GILBERT'S PLANS. - 131 -

CHAPTER XXX. GILBERT BECOMES A NEWSBOY. - 134 -

CHAPTER XXXI. GILBERT'S SECOND DAY. - 138 -

CHAPTER XXXII. A NOVEL PROPOSITION. - 142 -

CHAPTER XXXIII. THE NEW PROFESSOR. - 146 -

CHAPTER XXXIV. THE BROKER'S RETURN. - 152 -

CHAPTER XXXV. GILBERT'S TRIUMPH. - 157 -

CHAPTER XXXVI. MR. BRIGGS RETURNS FROM EUROPE. - 162 -

CHAPTER XXXVII. AN IMPORTANT REVELATION. - 166 -

CHAPTER XXXVIII. GILBERT'S SHIP COMES IN. - 170 -

CHAPTER XXXIX. CONCLUSION - 176 -

PREFACE.

"SHIFTING FOR HIMSELF" records the experiences of a boy who, in the course of a preparation for college, suddenly finds himself reduced to poverty. He is obliged to leave his books, and give up his cherished plans. How cheerfully Gilbert Greyson accepted the situation, and settled down to regular work, what obstacles he encountered and overcame, and what degree of success he met with in the end, the reader of this story will learn.

Though it must be admitted that Gilbert was more fortunate than the majority of boys in his position, it is claimed that he displayed qualities which may wisely be imitated by all boys who are called upon toshift for themselves. In the last three years many thousand American boys have been compelled, like Gilbert, to give up their cherished hopes, and exchange school-life for narrow means and hard work. Nothing is more uncertain than riches; and such cases are liable to occur at all times. I shall be glad if the story of Gilbert Greyson and his fortunes gives heart or hope to any of my young readers who are similarly placed. The loss of wealth often develops a manly self-reliance, and in such cases it may prove a blessing in disguise.

NEW YORK, Oct. 20, 1876.

CHAPTER I.

TWO SCHOOL-FELLOWS.

DR. BURTON'S boarding-school was in a ferment of hope and expectation. To-morrow was the end of the term, and vacation, so dear to the heart of every school-boy, was close at hand.

The school was not a large one. There were twenty-four boarding pupils, and an equal number of day-scholars from the village of Westville, in which the school had been established twenty years before. It was favorably situated, being only forty miles from New York. Half the boarding-scholars were from the city, and half from more distant places. Generally two or three pupils were sent to college each year, and, as the principal was a thorough scholar, maintained a creditable, often a high rank.

The school-session was over, and the boys separated into little knots. The day-scholars mostly went home, carrying their books under their arms.

Among the little knots we must direct particular attention to two boys, one a boarding-scholar, the other a day-scholar. The first was Gilbert Greyson, a handsome, spirited boy of sixteen; the other, John Munford, of about the same age, and much more plainly dressed. John was the son of a carpenter, of limited means, and had already begun to learn his father's business. But the father was sensible of the advantages of education, and had permitted his son to spend six months of each year at school, on condition that he would work the balance of the time. This arrangement seemed fair to John, and he took care, whether he studied or worked, to do both in earnest.

"How do you feel about vacation, John?" asked Gilbert.

"I was in no hurry to have it come, Gilbert. It is likely to be a very long vacation to me."

"How so?"

"I have got through my school-life."

"What! Are you not coming back next term?" asked Gilbert, with evident disappointment, for John was his most intimate friend.

"Neither next term, nor any other term, Gilbert, I am sorry to say."

"Have you finished your education, then?"

"So far as school goes."

"I am sorry for that. I shall miss you more than any one else."

"We shall still meet, I hope. I shall be at work; but there will be times—in the evening—when we can see each other."

"No doubt; but that won't be like sitting at the same desk, and studying together. You had better let me ask your father to send you one more year."

John shook his head.

"No, Gilbert, it ought not to be. My father is poor you know, and it has been a sacrifice to him to spare me half the year thus far. Now I must go to work in earnest, and perfect myself in my trade, that I may relieve him of all expense on my account."

"I suppose you are right, John; but I shall miss you none the less. Somehow I never could be reconciled to your becoming a carpenter. You are not cut out for it."

"Don't you think I will make a good one?" asked John, smiling.

"I am sure you will; but that isn't the question. Do you think you are better fitted for that than for anything else?"

"No, I don't."

"Do you prefer that trade to any other business?"

"No; but I can't choose for myself. I should rather be a teacher, or a lawyer; but there is small chance for either. For either I should be obliged to study years, and I can't afford to do that. A carpenter I am to be, and I will try to make a good one. Now, your case is different. You are going to school next year, I suppose?"

"Yes, I suppose so. That is as my guardian determines, and no letter has been received from him yet. I believe Dr. Burton is expecting one to-day or to-morrow."

"You won't spend the summer here, I suppose, Gilbert?"

"I am hoping to make a little tour, as I did last year."

"You went to the White Mountains then."

"Yes, and had a jolly good time."

"Where will you go this year?"

"I want to go to Niagara, stopping on the way at Saratoga. I have estimated that I can do it for a hundred dollars,—the same that my last summer's trip cost me."

"It must be splendid to travel," said John, enthusiastically. "I mean to see something of the world some day, though I suspect that I shall be a pretty old boy before I am able to. I have no guardian to send me money. I must earn my money before I spend it."

"I never earned a dollar in my life," said Gilbert. "I wonder how it would seem if I had to support myself, and make my own way in the world."

"It would seem hard at first. It comes natural to me; but then I have been differently brought up from you."

"I rather envy you, John," said Gilbert, thoughtfully. "You are so much more self-reliant, so much better able to take care of yourself."

"It's the difference in the training, Gilbert. I've no doubt it's in you; but circumstances have never brought it out. You expect to go to Yale College a year hence, don't you?"

"I expect to; at least that has been Dr. Burton's plan; but my guardian has never expressed his opinion. He has simply given his consent to my pursuing the course preparatory to entrance. I presume I shall go, however."

"What sort of a man is your guardian?"

"I have never seen much of him. He lives in the city, you know; but he never seemed to care to have me in his home much. He is a merchant, and appears to be wealthy. At any rate, he lives in a fine house up-town, and keeps up a good style of living."

"Who appointed him your guardian?"

"I don't know. I suppose my father."

"Is your father living?"

"I don't know."

"Don't know!" exclaimed John, opening his eyes.

"It seems strange to you; but I cannot give any explanation. My guardian tells me I shall know some time; meanwhile I am to ask no questions."

"Did that satisfy you?"

"No; but when I pressed my question I was silenced. I was told that I must be satisfied with being so well provided for, without trying to penetrate into matters that did not concern me."

"I should think it did concern you."

"So I do think; but there is no use in thinking about it. It would only perplex me to no purpose."

"I can't put myself in your place at all. To me it seems so natural to have a father and mother, and sister. How lonely you must feel!"

"I have never been used to them. And that makes a difference. Sometimes, to be sure, I begin to think over the matter and wish that I had ties like other boys; but it doesn't last long. But here we are at your home."

"Come in a minute, Gilbert."

"I don't know if I ought. I shall be late to supper, and the doctor wouldn't like that."

"Take supper with us."

"Yes, take supper with us," echoed John's mother, a pleasant, motherly-looking woman, who heard her son's words of invitation as he opened the door.

Gilbert hesitated.

The little table spread for tea looked so much more comfortable and home-like than the long table at the doctor's, that he was strongly tempted.

"We may not have as nice a supper as the doctor," continued Mrs. Munford, "but you may not mind that for once."

"You give the doctor's table too much credit," said Gilbert, smiling. "He doesn't mean to pamper any of us, or make us gluttons. I would a great deal rather take supper here."

"Then stay, Gilbert."

"I will," said Gilbert, in a tone of quick decision. "If the doctor scolds, why let him."

"He won't feel anxious about your not being back, will he?" asked Mrs. Munford.

"No; he knows I can take pretty good care of myself. Besides, it will be a saving to him, all the more because I have a very good appetite."

All laughed, for Dr. Burton, though on the whole a very worthy man, had the reputation of being what New Englanders call close. It was thought that he was more economical than he needed to be. At any rate he had made his school profitable, and was assessed for a very considerable sum in the list of village property-holders.

"How do you do, Mary?" said Gilbert, offering his hand to a girl of ten, John's sister, who just then entered the room.

"Pretty well," said Mary, shyly.

"Don't blush so, Mary," said John, teasing her as brothers are apt to do.

"I wasn't blushing," said Mary, indignantly.

"Just because Gilbert spoke to you."

"You are too bad, John," said his mother.

"How soon will supper be ready, mother?" asked John.

"In half an hour. Why; are you very impatient?"

"No; but I thought there might be time for Gilbert and me to have a catch in the yard."

"I'll tell you of a better way of filling up your time."

"What is that?"

"I am almost out of wood. Can't you saw me up a little?"

"I am afraid it will be dull to Gilbert to look on," said John.

"I don't propose to look on. You shall saw, and I will split."

"I don't like to set a visitor to work," said Mrs. Munford. "I didn't expect you to work for your supper."

"I shall enjoy it all the more. Come along, John. You'll see what execution I will make with your wood-pile."

As the two boys passed out into the woodshed, Mrs. Munford said, "I like Gilbert. Though he is rich, he doesn't put on any airs, but makes himself at home even among such plain people as we are."

CHAPTER II.

THE GUARDIAN'S LETTER.

WHEN supper was over, the boys took a walk, bringing round by the large square house occupied by Dr. Burton for his boarding-school. They had got within a few rods when John observed one of the younger boys running towards them.

"There's little Evans," he said. "He looks as if he had a message for you, Gilbert."

"From the doctor, I suppose. I'm in for a scolding, probably."

By this time Evans had reached them.

"You're wanted, Greyson," he said. "Why weren't you home to supper?"

"Is the doctor mad?"

"I don't know. He seems anxious to see you."

"All right. Then I'll go in. I must bid you good-night, John. Business before pleasure, you know, or rather business after pleasure."

"I hope the business won't be serious."

"I hope not. Good-night."

"Good-night, Gilbert."

There was a small room about twelve feet square, which was known as Dr. Burton's study. There was a desk beside the window, and book-shelves occupying the sides of the room. Hither it was that refractory or disobedient pupils were summoned, to receive admonition from the principal. In his early experience as teacher he had employed a sterner sort of discipline, but later he had substituted words for blows—very wisely, as I think.

Gilbert went at once to the doctor's study.

Dr. Burton was a tall, spare man, with strongly marked features, and on the whole rather a stern face. He looked toward the door as Gilbert opened it.

"Good-evening, sir," said Gilbert.

"You were absent from supper without notice or permission, Greyson," the doctor began.

"Yes, sir."

"Where were you?"

"I walked home with John Munford, and was invited to take supper there."

"I should have had no objection, if you had asked me. John Munford is one of my most reliable pupils, both in study and deportment."

Gilbert was pleased at this commendation of his friend.

"I hope you will excuse me for absence without permission," he said, apologizing with a good grace.

"You are excused, Greyson."

Supposing that the interview was over, Gilbert bowed, and was about to leave the room, but was stopped by the doctor.

"Stay," he said; "I have something more to say to you."

"What else have I done?" thought Gilbert, in surprise.

"Sit down," said the teacher.

Gilbert seated himself.

"How long have you been here, Greyson?"

"Six years, sir."

"In a year more you would be ready for college," said the doctor, musing.

"Why does he say 'would'? Why not 'will'?" thought Greyson.

"Am I to go to college?" asked Gilbert.

"I thought it probable; but I have just learned that your guardian has other views for you."

"Have you a letter from my guardian?" asked Gilbert, eagerly.

"Yes; it only reached me this afternoon. Would you like to read it?"

"Very much, sir."

"Here it is," said Dr. Burton, opening his desk, and drawing therefrom a letter enclosed in a buff envelope.

Gilbert quickly reached out for it.

This was the material portion of the letter, which Gilbert read with hurried interest:—

"Circumstances will not permit my ward remaining with you another year. I may say plainly that, should he do so, I should be compelled to defray the expense out of my own pocket, and consideration for my own family will not justify me in doing that. I have never, as you know, promised positively that he should go to college. It was barely possible that funds would be forthcoming which would admit of such a course; but it is now quite certain that there is no chance of it.

"He has already, as I should judge from your letters, considerably more than an average education,—more, indeed, than I had when I began my career,—and he ought to be satisfied with that. He has led an easy life hitherto. Now it is time that he did something for himself. Upon receipt of this letter, will you, as soon as may be, send him to me in New York? I will then confer with him as to his future plans."

This letter was signed Richard Briggs.

Gilbert read it with a mixture of feelings. He was making an unpleasant discovery. Though he knew little about his own affairs, he had always cherished the idea that he had considerable property, and that his path in life would be smoothed as only money can smooth it. He was not especially fond of money, nor did he ever presume on its supposed possession, but it was certainly comfortable to think that he was not poor.

Now it appeared that he had been all his life under a mistake. He was not a favored child of fortune after all, but a poor boy,—as poor, very likely, as his friend John Munford, from whom he had just parted. No wonder he looked with some bewilderment in the doctor's face when he had completed reading the letter.

The doctor, though a stern man, felt for the boy's disappointment. He, too, had been under the impression that Gilbert was at least comfortably provided for.

"Well, Greyson," he said, "I suppose this letter surprises you."

"Yes, sir, it does," answered Gilbert, slowly. "I always supposed that I had money to depend upon."

"I don't like to reflect upon your guardian, but it seems to me he ought to have apprised you beforehand of what you had to expect."

"I wish he had."

"Do you feel very much disappointed?" asked the doctor, eying his pupil with interest.

"Considerably, sir. It is hard to fancy myself a poor boy, with my own way to make in the world."

"It might have been worse. You have, as your guardian suggests, more than an average education."

"Thanks to you, sir."

"And to your own application," added the doctor, gratified by this tribute.

"I am glad you think so, sir. I hope it will help me in life."

"Undoubtedly it will. Besides, you will have the influence of your guardian to assist you. He will probably procure you a good place in some counting-room."

"I wish he had told me something about myself; where the money came from which had paid my bills hitherto."

Gilbert looked inquiringly at the doctor, as if to ask whether he could throw any light upon these points. But he was destined to be disappointed, for the doctor said, "He has not seen fit to take me into his confidence. I know no more than you do on this subject. Perhaps, in your approaching interview with him, he may give you information on the subject."

"I will ask him, at all events," said Gilbert. "When do you think it best that I should leave, Dr. Burton?"

"He wishes you to be sent 'as soon as may be,'" said the doctor, consulting the letter. "I should think you had better go to-morrow, or the next day."

"I will go to-morrow," said Gilbert, promptly.

"Can you get ready so soon?"

"I will pack to-night, sir."

"That shall be as you wish. If you would prefer to wait till another day, you can of course do so."

"Thank you, sir; but I want to see my guardian as soon as possible. Will you permit me, as the cars start early to-morrow, to go to-night, and bid good-by to John Munford?"

Under ordinary circumstances Dr. Burton would have declined this application, but he felt that it was only natural, and he gave the required permission without hesitation.

John Munford was astonished when, on opening the front door, he saw the school-fellow from whom he had so recently parted.

"What's the matter, Gilbert?" he asked; "has anything happened?"

"Yes," answered Gilbert. "Get your hat and take a walk with me. I'll tell you on the way."

CHAPTER III.

RICHARD BRIGGS.

GILBERT told his story briefly.

"So you see," he said in conclusion, "my position is like yours, after all. I am thrown upon my own exertions, and must face the world, without the help of money."

"I'm truly sorry," said John, in a tone of sympathy.

"Thank you, John; I knew you would be; but do you know, I am not sure whether I am so very sorry myself."

"But it must be hard for you to give up the hope of wealth."

"I needn't give up the hope," said Gilbert, "only if the hope is to be realized I shall have to make it for myself. As far as that goes I am no worse off than you; but there is one advantage you have over me."

"You are a better scholar than I am."

"I don't mean that. You have a father and mother and sister to encourage you, while I have no one."

"You have a friend, Gilbert; but he can't help you much."

"I know that, old fellow. You have been my most intimate friend for the last three years, and I hope and believe that our friendship is going to last. But I can't help feeling alone in the world."

"Why don't you ask your guardian about your father?"

"I mean to; but I don't believe he will tell me."

"Have you any idea what views he has for you?"

"Not the slightest. I suppose he will provide me with a place somewhere."

"Then you are entirely in the dark as to your prospects?"

"Entirely so."

"I wish you would write to me, Gilbert, after you are settled. I shall want to know all about it."

"I will certainly write. In fact, you will be my only correspondent. You must write me about yourself, too."

"There won't be much to write. My life will be uneventful. But you may like to hear news of the village and the school, that is, after vacation is over. I'll write all that I think will interest you."

"Thank you. You may be sure I shall want to hear. And now, John, I must bid you good-night, and good-by, for I am to start early in the morning, and have not yet packed my trunk."

"Good-night, then. Take care of yourself, Gilbert."

"The same to you, John."

So the two boys parted, but they saw each other once more. As Gilbert was about to get into the cars, John came up hurriedly and gave him a farewell shake of the hand.

"He's a capital fellow," thought Gilbert. "I hope he'll have good luck, and that we shall meet again soon."

An hour and a half brought our hero to the city. He stepped upon the platform, and getting upon a horse-car rode down-town to his guardian's office. He had a check for his trunk, but did not claim it at once, not feeling certain what would be his destination.

In a busy street, not five minutes' walk from Wall Street, was the office of Richard Briggs. Gilbert had no trouble in finding it, for he had been there before. Now, however, he had a new feeling as he entered the handsomely fitted-up room. He was no longer the wealthy ward, but as it appeared the humble dependent of the rich merchant whom he was to meet. The change was not an agreeable one, but he had made up his mind that he must face whatever was disagreeable in his position in a manly way.

"Is Mr. Briggs in?" he inquired, of a clerk who was writing at a desk.

"Yes; but I don't know if he will see you."

"He sent for me."

"Oh, did he? Well, he's in there."

The clerk pointed to an inner room, partitioned off from the main office.

Gilbert approached it, and as the door was partially open entered, and, removing his hat, said, "Good-morning, Mr. Briggs."

Mr. Briggs was a short man, inclined to be corpulent, with marked features.

He turned as he heard Gilbert's salutation.

"So you received my letter," he said.

"Dr. Burton did."

"Yes, I wrote to him. It's all the same."

"I thought I had better come up at once, sir."

"You did right."

"I was rather surprised at what your letter contained. Dr. Burton let me read it."

"You fancied yourself rich?" said the merchant, coldly.

"Yes, sir; I had always been led to suppose so."

"I never told you so."

"You did not tell me I was poor, and would have to make my own way."

"You complain of that, do you?" demanded Mr. Briggs, frowning.

"I wish I had known it before."

"It wasn't necessary to tell you. As to that, my judgment is of course superior to yours. You understand, do you, that you must now go to work?"

"I am ready, sir."

"Have you improved your time while at school?"

"Dr. Burton could tell you better than I as to that."

"He would be more reliable, of course. Still you must have some idea. Give me your own impressions. If you misrepresent, I shall find you out."

"I shall not misrepresent, sir."

"Of course not," said Mr. Briggs, ironically. "I suppose you were a model scholar."

"No; I was not; but I think I did pretty well."

"What do you know?"

"I can tell you how far I have been in my studies. I have been so far in Latin and Greek that in another year—perhaps less—I should be prepared for Yale College."

"You won't go there. You can't expect me to pay your expenses."

"I don't," said Gilbert, promptly. "I was only trying to give you an idea of what I knew."

"Very well. Are you good in arithmetic?"

"Yes, sir."

"How far have you been?"

"Through the book."

"That is well. How do you write?"

"Shall I give you a specimen of my writing, sir?"

"Yes. Here is a pen. Write anything you like. You may copy the first three lines of this newspaper article."

Gilbert did so.

"That will do very well. You don't write rapidly enough, but you will in time. I shall get you a place as soon as possible. Where is your trunk?"

"At the depot."

"You can have it sent to my house. You will stay there till I can get you a boarding-place or make some other arrangement for you. Do you know where I live?"

"Yes, sir."

"Give your check to an expressman, and tell him to bring it round. Stay, here is my son. I will put you in his charge."

A boy, about Gilbert's age, had just entered the office. He was the counterpart of his father, and no one could be likely to mistake the relationship. He glanced at Gilbert, but did not speak.

"Randolph, this is Gilbert Greyson," said his father.

"Good-morning," said Randolph, curtly. "Father, I want five dollars."

"What for? It seems to me you are always wanting money."

"Everybody needs money," said the son, pertly. "I want to go to a matinée this afternoon."

"I want you to go with Gilbert; he is going to stop with us a short time."

"He's old enough to take care of himself," said Randolph, unpleasantly.

"I can get along by myself," said Gilbert, quickly. "I don't want to trouble your son."

There was no great self-denial in this. It did not seem to our hero that he should particularly enjoy Randolph's companionship.

"At any rate you can go with him to the office of Adams' Express. He wants to send for his trunk."

"Will you give me the five dollars, then?"

"Here it is. Don't come again for a week."

"All right. Come along, whatever your name is."

This last polite invitation was addressed to our hero, who answered, shortly, "My name is Gilbert Greyson."

"Well, come along. I'm in a hurry."

When they had reached the street, Randolph's curiosity led him to say, "I thought you were at school."

"So I was; but your father sent for me."

"He's your guardian, isn't he?"

"So I thought; but he tells me I have no money, and must work for my living."

"Oh, indeed!" said Randolph, superciliously. "That's quite a different matter."

Gilbert didn't like his tone, but did not want to quarrel without cause.

They walked on without further conversation.

Presently Randolph said, "There's the express office. Now you can look after yourself."

He darted off, and Gilbert entered the office, not sorry to be rid of his uncongenial companion.

CHAPTER IV.

GILBERT MAKES A NEW ACQUAINTANCE.

HAVING arranged about his trunk, Gilbert took one of the University-Place cars at the Astor House, and rode up-town. Mrs. Briggs might not know of his coming, and the trunk might be refused.

The house was a four-story brown-stone front, with English basement, differing in no wise from the thousands of fashionable mansions to be seen in the upper part of the city.

Gilbert rang the bell.

"Is Mrs. Briggs at home?" he inquired of the servant, who answered the bell.

"I don't know, sir. I'll see. Will you send your name?"

Gilbert drew out a neat visiting-card bearing his name. The servant took it, and carried it to her mistress.

"Take a seat in the parlor, sir," she said, on her return. "Mrs. Briggs will be down directly."

The large parlor was showily furnished, in the regulation style. There was a chilly splendor about it that carried with it no idea of comfort or home feeling. Gilbert's attention was drawn to a family portrait near the front windows. There were three figures,—Mr. Briggs, Randolph, and a lady, who was probably Mrs. Briggs. She had a high forehead, a thin face, cold blue eyes, and pinched lips. Gilbert privately decided that he should not like the original of that portrait.

While he was examining it Mrs. Briggs entered.

"Mr. Greyson?" she asked, in a chilly way.

"Yes, madam."

"I believe I have not met you before. You are Mr. Briggs' ward or protégé?"

"Yes, madam."

"I thought you were at a boarding-school somewhere in the country."

"So I have been, madam; but the term is at an end, and Mr. Briggs sent for me to come to the city."

"Indeed! Have you seen Mr. Briggs this morning?"

"Yes, madam. It is by his direction that I have ordered my trunk brought here."

The lady arched her eyebrows slightly.

"Then you propose to favor us with a visit," she said.

There was a slight emphasis on the word favor, which Gilbert felt to be a sneer.

"I am at Mr. Briggs' disposal," he answered. "He ordered me to come here first. I hope I may not give you any trouble."

"Oh, no; you will excuse my remaining with you—I have an engagement. I will tell the servants to receive your trunk, and put it in your room. Our lunch will be ready at one o'clock."

"Thank you," said Gilbert, hastily; "I think I shall not be here at lunch. I want to go about the city."

It was eleven o'clock; and he was sure he could not kill the time in that frigid parlor for two hours.

"Very well," said Mrs. Briggs; "then we shall see you at dinner. Our dinner-hour is six."

"Thank you, madam."

"If you come earlier, you can ask to be shown to your room."

Gilbert thanked her again.

"Now I must leave you. Good-morning."

Mrs. Briggs sailed out of the room, and Gilbert, following her, let himself out into the street.

"So that's what they call a city mansion," he said to himself. "I'd ten times rather be in my room at Dr. Burton's. I felt as if I was in danger of stifling in that showy parlor. I hope I am not going to live there."

Gilbert had nowhere to go; but the city was a novelty, and he wandered about the streets, looking about him with the keen interest of a country visitor.

A short walk brought him to the Fifth Avenue Hotel. He had heard of it often, but never seen the interior. Attracted by curiosity he went in. He took a seat near the door, and idly watched the people who were continually going out and coming in. Among the latter he soon saw a familiar face. Randolph Briggs lounged in, swinging a light cane.

"Hallo!" he said, noticing Gilbert, "you here!"

"So it seems," said Gilbert.

"You aint going to stop here, are you?"

"For the present, I am staying at your house."

"Oh, yes, I forgot. Been up there?"

"Yes."

"Did you see mother?"

"For a few minutes."

"Didn't she invite you to lunch?"

"Yes; but I thought I should like to look round the city a little."

"What do you expect to do?"

"I suppose I must get a place. As I have no property, I must do something to earn my living."

"You don't expect to stay at our house, do you?"

"I don't expect anything. I feel bound to be guided by your father."

"You see it would be awkward to have an office-boy at our table, meeting our friends."

"I suppose so," said Gilbert, his lip curling.

"It wouldn't be proper."

"I suppose you know best."

"Probably father will find you some cheap boarding-house. That will be better for you, you know."

"It's a pity you were not my guardian," said Gilbert.

"Why?"

"Because you seem to understand so well what is best for me."

Randolph looked puzzled. Was this penniless boy chaffing him, or was he in earnest? Randolph's vanity led him to think the latter.

"Yes, of course I do. I've lived in the city all my life. I ought to know what's what. Do you play billiards?"

"No; I never learned."

"There's a billiard-room below. I thought we might have a game."

"I never played a game in my life."

"Then there would be no fun for me. I guess I'll go in and get a drink. Are you thirsty?"

"No, thank you."

"I'm going to the theatre afterwards—a matinée. I've only got one ticket, but you can buy one at the door."

"Thank you; I would rather walk about the streets this afternoon."

Randolph lounged into the bar-room, ordered his drink, then lounged out again.

He nodded carelessly to Gilbert as he went out.

"See you by and by," he said.

Gilbert bowed.

"It doesn't strike me I shall like that boy," he said to himself. "I wonder if his father knows about his drinking."

Gilbert amused himself for a little while longer watching those who entered and departed from the great hotel. Then he went out into the street, and proceeded down Broadway. He made slow progress, for there was much to interest a stranger like himself in the busy life of the street. At length it occurred to him that he would go to Central Park, of which he had heard a great deal. By this time he had strayed to Sixth Avenue and Fourteenth Street.

At the same time with Gilbert a young girl of thirteen entered the car, and, as chance would have it, she and our hero were seated side by side.

Presently the conductor made his rounds.

First he presented his hand for the young girl's fare. She felt in her pocket, but apparently in vain. Her face flushed, and she looked very much embarrassed.

"I think I forgot to bring my money," she murmured. "I will get out."

"By no means," said Gilbert, promptly. "Permit me to pay your fare. For two," he said, handing a ten-cent stamp to the conductor.

"You are very kind," said the young girl, looking relieved. "I live in Forty-eighth Street, and should not have liked to walk so far. I am sure I can't tell how I happened to forget my money; I am ever so much obliged to you."

"Oh, don't mention it," said Gilbert, privately thinking his new acquaintance one of the prettiest girls he had ever met.

"Will you give me your name and residence," she asked, "that I may send you the money?"

"With pleasure, on condition that you won't think of repaying such a trifle," said Gilbert.

He drew out a card, added his guardian's residence, and passed it to his companion.

"At any rate," said the young girl, "you must call, and let mamma thank you for your politeness to me. This is mine."

She handed Gilbert a petite card, with the name of

"LAURA VIVIAN,

"No. — West th Street."

"Thank you," said Gilbert. "I will call with pleasure, but not to receive thanks."

After this the two young people continued to converse with a freedom upon which they would not have ventured if older and more conventional; and Gilbert was really sorry when his fair companion arrived at her street and got out.

CHAPTER V.

AT THE DINNER-TABLE.

AT five o'clock Gilbert started from the park, where he had sauntered about for several hours, and reached the house of Mr. Briggs half an hour or more before dinner.

"Your room is ready," said the servant, who had received her instructions. "Shall I show you the way up?"

"If you please. Has my trunk come?"

"Yes, sir."

"The dinner-hour is six, I believe."

"Yes, sir. The bell will ring at that time."

Gilbert understood that he was expected to remain in his room till dinner-time. That, however, would have been his choice.

He followed the servant to a small hall-bedroom on the third floor, where he found his trunk awaiting him. He opened it, and, taking out his comb and brush, and a clean collar, made his dinner toilet. A new life had opened before him, and he could not help wondering what it would be like. In the midst of his meditations came the sound of the bell, and he went downstairs.

Mr. Briggs was already present.

"Well," said he, stiffly, "so you found your way here?"

"Yes, sir."

"Did you see Mrs. Briggs?"

"Yes, sir."

"And how have you spent the day?"

"I spent the afternoon at Central Park."

"Was Randolph with you?"

"No, sir. It wasn't necessary; I found my way without any trouble."

Here Mrs. Briggs entered.

She nodded slightly to Gilbert, and said, in a chilly way:—

"Take that seat, Mr. Greyson."

Gilbert seated himself, and Randolph, who entered directly afterwards, sat down opposite.

"You were not with Gilbert to-day, Randolph," said his father.

"No, sir."

"Where were you?"

"At the theatre."

"Humph! you go to the theatre too much."

"How can you say so, Mr. Briggs?" said the mother, who, though her heart was cold to all beside, fairly idolized her son, and as a consequence foolishly indulged him.

"This is the second time he has been this week."

"The boy is young, and needs recreation."

"It seems to me it is all recreation with him, and no work. When I was a boy, I was lucky if I could go to a place of amusement once in three months."

"You hadn't got a rich father," said Randolph.

"I am not made of money," muttered Mr. Briggs, "though you seem to think I am."

"Really, Mr. Briggs," said his wife, "it is ridiculous to expect Randolph to spend as little as you did when you were a boy. The circumstances are quite different."

Mr. Briggs frowned, but did not answer.

"What did you do with yourself?" asked Randolph, turning to Gilbert.

"I went to Central Park. It is a beautiful place."

"I never go there," said Randolph. "You meet only low persons there."

"I saw many driving about in handsome carriages. Are they low?"

"Of course not. I meant only low persons walk there."

"Randolph is right," said his mother.

"Still I think I shall go again," said Gilbert.

"Oh, it's different with you. You are a poor boy, aint you?" said Randolph, bluntly.

Gilbert colored a little.

"I only know what your father has told me," said he.

"Have you got any property of Gilbert's, father?" asked Randolph.

"This is not the time to ask such questions," said his father, looking annoyed.

"Why not? There is no company—no one but ourselves."

"Ahem!" said Mr. Briggs, clearing his throat: "there was a very small property, but it has all been spent on Gilbert's education."

"Who left him the property?" asked Randolph, persistently.

Gilbert was interested in the answer to this question, and he looked with eager inquiry at his guardian, hoping that he would reveal what he had so long desired to know.

"You are very curious," said Mr. Briggs, displeased.

"There's no reason why you shouldn't tell me; is there, father?"

"No," answered his father, slowly. "The money was left him by his father, who was an old schoolmate of mine. He died in the West Indies, and sent me the money in trust for his son, to provide for him as long as it lasted. It was exhausted nearly a year since, but I kept Gilbert at school till now at my own expense. Now the time has come when he must shift for himself."

"Rather hard on you, Gilbert," said Randolph.

"I am willing to look out for myself," said Gilbert, quietly. "My father did all he could for me. I have a good education, thanks partly to you, Mr. Briggs, and I ought to be able to make my way."

"Oh, you are welcome," said Mr. Briggs, rather uncomfortably.

"You have done more than could have been expected, Mr. Briggs," said his wife. "Why did you not take the boy from school months ago?"

"I wanted him to have a fair education."

"It seems to me he was already sufficiently educated for his sphere in life," said the lady. "I don't believe in educating persons beyond their station."

There was something in the lady's remarks which grated harshly upon the ear of our young hero. What right had Mrs. Briggs to assume that his station was inferior to hers? The dislike which he had already begun to entertain for her was increased. He found it impossible to like any of the family, but he had insight enough to see that in cold selfishness Mrs. Briggs exceeded her husband and son.

"It seems to me," said Mr. Briggs, in answer to his wife's last remark, "that a good education is a good thing for any one to possess, be he rich or poor."

"You wouldn't advise a boy that was going to be a mechanic to study Latin or Greek, would you?"

"If he liked it."

"Then I can't agree with you," retorted the lady, sharply; "I consider it simply time and money thrown away."

"Have you studied Latin and Greek, Gilbert?" asked Randolph.

"Yes."

"Have you gone far in them?"

"In a year I should have been ready to enter Yale College."

"And after all I suppose you will be a mechanic."

"Why should I be?" demanded Gilbert.

"You have no money."

"I suppose there are other kinds of business I can learn."

"Perhaps so."

Apparently tiring of the subject, Randolph turned to his mother.

"Has any invitation come for me?" he asked.

"Invitation—to what?"

"I hear that Laura Vivian is going to give a party. I didn't know but she might invite me."

"The Vivians do not visit us. I should be glad to become acquainted. They move in the very first society. Do you know Laura?"

"I knew her at dancing-school. I used to dance with her sometimes. She was a great favorite. All the boys wanted her for a partner."

"It is hardly likely she will invite you. I wish she would."

"What is the name of the young lady?" asked Gilbert, interested.

"Laura Vivian. What interest can you feel in her?"

"I made the young lady's acquaintance this afternoon," said Gilbert, quietly.

"Laura Vivian? Impossible."

"Doesn't she live in West Forty-eighth Street?"

"Yes."

"Then it is the same one, as you will see by this card."

Here Gilbert produced the card referred to in the last chapter.

"How on earth did you get acquainted with her?" exclaimed Mrs. Briggs. "Who introduced you?"

"I believe I introduced myself," said Gilbert, smiling. "I'll tell you all about it," and he recounted the circumstances of his acquaintance.

"She invited you to call?" exclaimed Randolph, enviously.

"Yes."

"Do you mean to go?"

"I shall go once, out of politeness."

"She will think you want to be repaid your five cents," said Mrs. Briggs, disagreeably.

"I don't think she will," said Gilbert. "At any rate I will take the risk."

"Will you take me with you?" asked Randolph.

"I hardly think it would be proper," said Gilbert; "but if I have a second invitation I may take the liberty of doing so."

"Gilbert is right," said Mr. Briggs.

Randolph was disappointed, and indulged in a sneer at a penniless boy like Gilbert calling on a young lady of high social position. But Gilbert did not choose to notice it.

CHAPTER VI.

HOW GILBERT GOT ON.

WHEN dinner was over, Gilbert found that he was not going to have the pleasure of Randolph's companionship.

"Where are you going, Randolph?" asked his father, as Randolph was leaving the room.

"I'm going out."

"Perhaps Gilbert may like to go with you," suggested Mr. Briggs.

"I've got an engagement," said Randolph, shortly.

"When was it made?"

"This afternoon."

"Don't let me interfere with Randolph's engagements," said Gilbert, hastily.

"Won't you feel lonely?" asked Mr. Briggs.

"Oh, no, sir. I shall take a walk down Broadway. There will be plenty to take up my attention."

"Randolph can hardly be expected to give up his engagement," said Mrs. Briggs. "I am surprised, Mr. Briggs, that you should expect it."

Mr. Briggs muttered something about politeness.

Gilbert protested again that he could get along very well by himself, and the matter dropped.

Presently he went out, and Mrs. Briggs, who had been waiting her opportunity, commenced an attack upon her husband.

"What are your plans for this boy, Mr. Briggs?" she asked. "Are you going to support him in idleness?"

"Certainly not. I shall find him a place as soon as I can."

"What claim has he upon you, I should like to know?"

"He has only me to look out for him."

"What of that?"

"He was the son of my old schoolmate."

"I have old schoolmates, too, and some, I suppose, are in want; but I am not going to adopt their children."

"This boy was especially recommended to me, and what property his father left was given in trust to me for him."

"Well, it's all used up, isn't it?"

"Yes."

"Then your trust is at an end."

"What are you driving at, wife?"

"I want to know whether you expect this boy to remain in your house."

"I see no objection."

"I do. You will be pampering him at the expense of your own son."

Mr. Briggs shrugged his shoulders.

"I apprehend," he said, "that our household expenses will not be increased materially by Gilbert's remaining here."

"Clothes and board cost something. Besides, he is not a fit companion for Randolph."

"Why not?"

"He is a poor boy."

"He has the education and manners of a young gentleman. It strikes me that he is quite the equal of Randolph in these respects."

"You are always ready to side against your own boy."

"I don't want to spoil him."

"You seem to prefer this new boy."

"Not at all. Must I be unjust to every other boy, because I have a son of my own?"

"You know what I mean well enough."

"The point seems to be, that you don't want Gilbert in the house."

"No."

"What shall I do with him?"

"Let him shift for himself."

Mr. Briggs shook his head.

"The world would talk," said Mr. Briggs.

"Let them talk!" said the lady, independently.

"It isn't best to incur the reproach of your fellow-men."

"Well, get him a cheap boarding-house: that's more suited to his station in life than a home like ours."

"Let him stay here a few days, and I will see what I can do."

Mrs. Briggs would have preferred to have Gilbert leave the next day, but decided to accept the concession made by her husband. He was placed in a difficult position, but did not venture to tell his wife all. The truth was, for I do not mean to make a mystery of it, he had wronged Gilbert most grievously. The sum of money placed in his hands in trust for our hero had been not a small sum, but seventy-five thousand dollars. Gilbert's father, trusting all to the honor of his friend, had exacted no guaranties of good faith. So far as Mr. Briggs knew, no living person was aware of the amount of Gilbert's inheritance. There was no one, so far as he knew, to contradict his assertion that it had all been expended in the education of our hero. Yet it troubled him. He had made up his mind to wrong the boy, but he was not so hardened as to do it without some qualms of conscience. He meant to do something for him, get him a place, and give him a home in his own family; but here, as we see, Mrs. Briggs had interfered with his plans. He could not make up his mind to throw Gilbert wholly upon his own resources, and he was disappointed at his wife's opposition. He was not wholly a bad man, but the temptation of appropriating Gilbert's money had been too great, and he had yielded. He had used it in his business, and a sudden call for it would have very much embarrassed him.

Meanwhile Gilbert set out on his walk. The crowded city streets, which had interested him in the daytime, assumed a new charm in the evening. Walking slowly along, looking in at the brilliantly lighted windows, he did not feel the need of companionship. In fact, he was rather glad that Randolph was not with him, for he had already satisfied himself that they had very little in common.

GILBERT MEETS MR. VIVIAN.

Half an hour had passed, when all at once he heard his name called.

"Good-evening, Mr. Greyson," said a sweet voice.

Turning quickly, he recognized Laura Vivian.

"Good-evening, Miss Vivian," he said, pleased at the meeting.

"Papa," said Laura, "this is Mr. Greyson, who was so polite to me in the cars."

Then for the first time Gilbert noticed that Laura was accompanied by a pleasant-looking gentleman of middle age.

"I am glad to meet you, Mr. Greyson," said Mr. Vivian, cordially. "My daughter has told me that you extricated her from a dilemma."

"It isn't worth mentioning, sir," said Gilbert. "I am ashamed to be thanked for such a little thing."

"It was a trifle, no doubt, but a mark of kind attention no less. My daughter and I are out for a walk. If you have no engagement, will you join us?"

"With great pleasure, sir," said Gilbert; and he spoke sincerely.

"Do you live in the city?" asked Mr. Vivian.

"I have been at a boarding-school hitherto, but I have now come to the city to live."

"Do your parents reside here?"

Gilbert looked sober.

"I have no parents," he said.

"Indeed!" said Mr. Vivian, in a voice of sympathy.

"Indeed I have no relatives that I am aware of; Mr. Richard Briggs, a merchant of this city, is my guardian."

"Richard Briggs? I know of him."

"I ought to say, however," added Gilbert, who did not wish to sail under false colors, "that I can hardly continue to call him my guardian, as he informs me that my little property has been all expended on my education, and that I am now penniless, and must work for my living."

"I don't consider that a misfortune," said Mr. Vivian. "It will make a man of you the sooner. But about this property, do you know how much it amounted to originally?"

"No, sir."

"Hasn't Mr. Briggs ever rendered an account to you?"

"No, sir. I have always supposed that I should be rich until within a week. Then, for the first time, I was told that I must withdraw from school, and get a place."

"Mr. Briggs has not treated you fairly in leaving you uninformed as to your real position," said Mr. Vivian, gravely.

"I won't blame him, but I wish he had told me earlier."

By this time they had reached a fashionable confectioner's.

"Come in with us, and have an ice-cream," said Mr. Vivian.

"Thank you, sir," said Gilbert, and the three entered and sat down at one of the small tables.

At a table near by sat Randolph Briggs. Looking up by chance, he was astonished to see his father's penniless ward in such company.

"By Jove!" he muttered, "that young beggar has more cheek than any one I know of."

He would have liked to have joined the party, but even he had not the assurance to force himself upon them. So he sat watchful and envious, his jealousy excited by the evident favor with which Gilbert was regarded.

"If Mr. Vivian knew he hadn't a cent in the world, he wouldn't be quite so cordial," he thought.

But Mr. Vivian did know. The trouble was that Randolph did not know him, or he would not have suspected him of such regard for wealth and its possession.

CHAPTER VII.

A SPITEFUL WOMAN.

RANDOLPH lost no time in going home to report what he had seen. Both his father and mother were surprised to see him back so soon.

"I am glad you came home early," said his mother.

"Did you see anything of Gilbert while you were out?" asked his father.

"Do you suppose, Mr. Briggs, that Randolph is going to follow your beggarly ward?" demanded Mrs. Briggs, sharply.

"He might have met him," said her husband, in an apologetic tone.

"I did meet him," said Randolph, in so significant a tone that both his father and mother looked at him for an explanation.

"Where do you think I saw him?" continued Randolph.

"In some low place," suggested his mother.

"Not at all. He was eating an ice-cream at Delmonico's."

"Pretty well for a penniless boy!" said Mrs. Briggs. "I suppose he expects us to supply him with money to pay for his extravagant outlays."

"Oh, he didn't pay for it himself. He got Mr. Vivian to treat him."

"Mr. Vivian!"

"Yes: he had picked up Mr. Vivian and Laura somewhere, and probably suggested going in to take an ice-cream."

"No doubt Mr. Vivian invited him," said Mr. Briggs, who did not allow dislike to run away with his common-sense.

"He is certainly the most forward and impudent boy I ever met," exclaimed Mrs. Briggs, whose annoyance arose largely from Gilbert's succeeding better with the Vivians than her own son.

"Really, my dear," expostulated her husband, "I am sure you do the boy injustice."

"Don't call me 'my dear,'" said Mrs. Briggs, scornfully. "I can't see what has got into you. You certainly must be wilfully blind if you don't see through the artfulness of that boy."

"What has he done?"

"He has wormed himself into the intimacy of Mr. Vivian; that is what he has done."

"Why shouldn't he? If Mr. Vivian is inclined to befriend him, it will be a saving to me."

"It won't be for long. Mr. Vivian will find him out, and cast him off."

"I don't know that there is anything in particular to find out. He seems to me as good as the average of boys."

"Well, Mr. Briggs, I can only say that you seem infatuated about him. I beg to say that I am not."

"That is apparent," said her husband, smiling.

"Moreover," added his wife, provoked, "I wish to tell you that it is disagreeable to me to have him in the house. So the sooner you can find a boarding-house for him the better."

"Well, I will, if you insist upon it."

"I do insist upon it."

"Then I will try in a day or two to find him a home."

"Mark my words, Mr. Briggs: you will find, sooner or later, that my prejudice against him is not so foolish as you imagine. That boy will turn out badly."

"I hope not."

"It's all very well hoping; but you'll see."

Randolph now got up to go.

"Where are you going, Randolph?" asked his mother.

"I am going out a while; I can't say where."

"Why can't you be satisfied to stay at home?"

"Oh, it's so stupid staying at home," said Randolph. "I want to go where there's something going on."

"It isn't a very good plan for a boy of your age to spend his evenings about the street," said Mr. Briggs.

"Why shouldn't he go out?" said Mrs. Briggs, in the spirit of opposition. "You haven't anything to say about your favorite being out."

"The city is new to him. If he went out every evening like Randolph, I should think it a bad plan."

"I suppose you would find some excuse for him."

"Really," said Mr. Briggs, "I shall be quite as anxious to get him out of the house as you, if you keep up such an incessant attack."

"If you are going to talk to me in this style, I will retire," said Mrs. Briggs, stiffly.

Suiting the action to the word, she rose and left the room. Her husband made no opposition. Indeed, as her temper was, he felt her withdrawal a relief. He settled himself down to the comfortable reading of an evening paper, and had about completed its perusal when the bell rang, and Gilbert entered the room.

"Well, Gilbert, did you have a pleasant time?" asked his guardian.

"Yes, sir; unexpectedly so. I met Mr. Vivian and his daughter, and went to Delmonico's with them."

"You found him an agreeable man, no doubt?"

"Yes, sir; he treated me very kindly for a stranger."

"He has a high reputation," said Mr. Briggs.

"Is he in business?"

"Yes; he is an importer, and is generally considered very wealthy. He is a prudent, conservative man, who avoids dangerous risks, and so meets with few losses."

"He has invited me to call next Friday evening at his house."

"You had better go, by all means. His friendship may be valuable to you."

"I am glad you approve of my going, for I am sure I shall enjoy it."

"Now, Gilbert," said Mr. Briggs, clearing his throat, "as we have a good opportunity, I will say a few words about my plans for you."

"I wish you would, sir. I am anxious to know what is to be my path in life."

"I propose to get you into some store or counting-room in the city."

"Yes, sir. That is what I should like."

"And," continued Mr. Briggs, rather embarrassed, "it will probably be necessary for you to obtain a boarding-place nearer the business part of the city than you would be here."

"I should think it would be better," said Gilbert, who decidedly preferred a boarding-house to an establishment presided over by Mrs. Briggs, who, he clearly saw, was not disposed to be his friend.

"We have breakfast too late to admit of your getting down-town in time," continued Mr. Briggs, who seemed to want to justify himself in the eyes of his ward for the inhospitable proposal.

"Yes, sir, I think it will be every way better," said Gilbert, promptly. "What wages do you think I can get, sir?"

"Why," said Mr. Briggs, hesitating, "beginners like you seldom command more than five dollars a week at first."

Gilbert looked serious.

"I suppose," he said, "this will not be enough to pay all my expenses."

"Certainly not," said his guardian, "but you need not feel troubled about that. I will make up the balance necessary till you are far enough advanced to be self-supporting."

"You are very kind, sir," said Gilbert, gratefully; "but it appears that I have already cost you considerable."

"Oh, that is of no consequence," said Mr. Briggs, hurriedly. "I was your father's friend, and naturally I feel an interest in your progress."

"Thank you, sir; but I don't like to be a continued burden to you. Do you think it will be long before I can support myself?"

"It will certainly be two years—perhaps three."

"Of course I don't know anything about it, but I should think my services ought to be worth my board and clothes before that."

"We must take things as we find them," said his guardian. "There are a dozen applicants for every place open to a boy, and while this state of things continues employers will pay low wages. Besides, it is felt that a boy is paid partly in the knowledge of business he acquires."

"I have no doubt you are right, sir; but how do poor boys manage who have no one to make up the deficiency?"

"Some of them have to live on five dollars a week."

"Couldn't I do it?"

"I should not be willing to have you. You have been brought up as a gentleman, and could not get along as well as if you had always been poor."

"I will trust to your judgment, sir; but I shall want you to keep an account of all you spend for me."

"Why?"

"Because some day I mean to repay it," said Gilbert, proudly.

"You are too particular about this matter," said Mr. Briggs, uncomfortably.

"No, sir, I don't think so. I think I am old enough now to undertake my entire support."

"I will see about it, then."

This closed the conversation for the evening. Gilbert was glad to have spoken to his guardian. Now he knew better what to look forward to.

CHAPTER VIII.

GILBERT GETS A PLACE.

THE next morning, about eight o'clock, the family were gathered about the breakfast-table. Randolph was ten minutes late. He came in looking sleepy and cross.

"Randolph," said his father, "what made you so late last evening?"

"I wasn't late."

"You may not call half-past eleven late; I do."

"It wasn't more than half-past ten when I came in."

"You are quite mistaken. I looked at my watch when I heard you coming upstairs."

"It was rather late; but you needn't make such a fuss about it, Mr. Briggs," said his wife. "You have been out later than that yourself."

"Whenever I have been late, I had a good reason for it. Besides, there is some difference in age between Randolph and myself."

"At any rate, you needn't scold him before a stranger."

"I do not consider Gilbert a stranger. Besides, what I say is partly meant for him. It is not wise for any boy of his or Randolph's age to remain out till nearly twelve."

"I hope you are almost through; I am getting tired of the subject."

Thus Mrs. Briggs gave Randolph indirect encouragement, by taking his part against his father.

Mr. Briggs shrugged his shoulders and was silent. Gilbert felt rather uncomfortable.

"Will you have some more coffee?" asked Mrs. Briggs, in an icy tone.

"No, thank you," he said.

"You may go down-town with me, Gilbert," said Mr. Briggs. "I will introduce you to a gentleman who will possibly give you a place."

"Thank you, sir."

"I hope, Mr. Briggs, you will bear in mind what I said last night," said his wife.

She referred to his getting a boarding-place for Gilbert.

"I have not forgotten it," he answered.

Gilbert and his guardian took a University Place car, and they rode down-town together.

Mr. Briggs obtained a seat, but Gilbert was compelled to stand, on account of the crowded state of the car.

Seated beside Mr. Briggs was a business man of about his own age.

"Good-morning, Mr. Sands," he said, for it was an acquaintance.

"Good-morning, Mr. Briggs. Is this young man your son?"

"No, he is under my charge, however. I have a son of about his age."

"Is he at school?"

"He has been till recently. I am looking for a place for him at present. It is time he commenced his business education."

"Indeed," said the gentleman, thoughtfully. "Are you thinking of any business in particular?"

"No. I shall accept any good opening for him."

"The fact is," said Sands, "I am looking for a boy to enter my own office. I was compelled yesterday to dismiss one who had been with me for six months, on account of dishonesty. I found he appropriated revenue-stamps, and sold them. I don't know how long this has been going on, but probably I have been a considerable loser."

"I don't think you will have any such difficulty with Gilbert, if you are inclined to take him," said Mr. Briggs.

"I like his appearance, and will take him at once, if you say so. I have been in the habit of paying five dollars a week."

"It is as much as I expected him to earn for the present. Gilbert, this gentleman is willing to give you a place in his office."

Gilbert had already formed a favorable opinion of Mr. Sands and he answered promptly, "I am very much obliged to him, and shall be glad to be in his employ."

Mr. Sands looked pleased.

"May I ask what is your business, sir?" continued Gilbert.

"I am a broker; my office is at No. — Wall Street."

"I am afraid you will find me very ignorant of business," said Gilbert; "but I hope to learn rapidly."

"There is nothing that will puzzle you at first. If you remain any length of time, there will be something to learn."

"I have assured Mr. Sands," said Mr. Briggs, "that he can rely upon your honesty. His last boy was discharged for lack of that very necessary quality."

"I don't think he will be disappointed in me, so far as that goes," said Gilbert, proudly.

"I don't think I shall," said the broker, upon whom Gilbert's modest but manly bearing had produced a very favorable impression. "When shall you be ready to go to work?"

"At any time, sir."

"Does that mean to-day?"

"Yes, sir."

"I will stipulate, however," said Mr. Briggs, "that Gilbert may be released at four o'clock. I want to select a boarding-place for him, and that will give me time."

"Oh, certainly," said the broker. "I can let him go earlier if you desire it."

"No, it will not be necessary; I shall not myself be at leisure till that hour. You know my place of business, Gilbert, do you not?"

"Yes, sir; I have been there already, you know."

"I remember. Very well, go with Mr. Sands to his office, and come to me at four this afternoon."

"Very well, sir."

It seemed rather strange to Gilbert to find himself already in a situation. The transition from life at school had been very sudden. On the whole he was not sorry for it. It kindled his ambition to think that he was going to make himself useful; that he was to have a part in the busy scene around him. He only regretted that for some time to come he could not hope to earn his living entirely; that for two or three years, perhaps, he was to be a source of expense to his guardian.

"I will be as economical as I can," he thought. "I will cost him as little as possible, and when I am older I will pay back every cent I owe him, if I am lucky enough to have the means."

Had Gilbert only known it, it was Mr. Briggs who was heavily in his debt, and the small sum which would be allowed him to help defray his expenses was already his own. It was just as well that he did not know it. It was better that he should feel entirely dependent upon his own exertions for support. To an active and ambitious boy it is a stimulus and an incentive to effort.

"What is your whole name, Gilbert?" asked Mr. Sands, pleasantly.

"Gilbert Greyson, sir."

"You have been at school until recently, Mr. Briggs tells me."

"Yes, sir."

"In the city?"

"No, sir; I was at Dr. Burton's classical school, in the town of Westville."

"I have heard of it. Did you pursue a classical course?"

"Yes, sir."

"Then you know something of Latin and Greek?"

"Yes, sir. In a year I should have been ready for Yale College."

"Then you already have more than an average education."

"I hoped to have a better, sir."

"You need not stop learning because you left school. It happens that I, myself, pursued a course similar to yours, and left my studies for business when nearly ready for college."

"Indeed, sir?" said Gilbert, interested.

"But I still keep up my Latin a little. Greek I have pretty much forgotten."

By this time they had reached the office of Mr. Sands. It was not large, but was neat and well furnished. A clerk was at a desk, engaged in writing. There was, besides, in waiting a boy of about Gilbert's age, who apparently wished to speak to Mr. Sands.

"You here, John?" demanded Mr. Sands.

"Yes, sir," whined the boy. "Won't you take me back, sir?"

The broker shook his head.

"No, I cannot," he said. "You have deceived me, and I cannot trust you."

"I won't do it again, sir."

"I could not take you back now if I would," said the broker. "I have engaged this boy in your place."

John scowled at Gilbert with a sense of personal injury, and left the office.

CHAPTER IX.

THE FIRST DAY IN BUSINESS.

DURING the day Gilbert learned the way to the Stock Exchange, to the bank where his employer kept an account, and to the Post Office. He was also sent on various errands to offices of other brokers and business men. Indeed, he was kept so busy that he found the day pass very rapidly. He made up his mind that he should like Mr. Sands, whose manner towards him was marked with kindness and consideration.

It was not so, however, with the clerk who has already been mentioned. He was disposed to regard Gilbert as an unwelcome intruder into the office. His prejudice will be understood when the reader learns that he was a cousin of the boy who had been discharged. He had interceded to have John reinstated in his place; but Mr. Sands had been inexorable.

"I should like to oblige you, Mr. Moore," said he, "but I cannot take back your cousin. I must have a boy in whom I can feel a reasonable degree of confidence."

"John has reformed, sir. He will be strictly honest hereafter."

"I hope he will, for his own sake; but it is best for him to find some place where there will be fewer opportunities to steal."

The clerk saw that it would be of no use to pursue the subject further, and was silent. But he made up his mind to dislike any boy that might come in his cousin's place.

In his employer's presence he did not venture to manifest his feelings, but when Gilbert came back from an errand later in the day, Mr. Sands being absent at the Board, he said irritably, "What made you so long?"

"So long?" repeated Gilbert, in surprise. "I lost no time, Mr. Moore. I went directly to the office where I was sent, and as soon as my business was attended to I came directly back."

"Oh, no doubt!" sneered Moore. "You didn't stop to play on the way, *of course.*"

"No, I didn't," said Gilbert, indignantly.

"Then you stopped to hear a hand-organ, or something of the kind," persisted Moore, in a disagreeable manner.

"You are quite mistaken, Mr. Moore. You probably know where the office is, and must be aware that I had no time for any such delay."

"Oh, you are a model boy, I have no doubt!" sneered the clerk.

"I have great doubts on the subject myself," said Gilbert, good-naturedly. "I never had that reputation."

"Did you ever do anything wrong?"

"No doubt I have."

"I thought perhaps you were intending to pass yourself off as an angel."

"I don't believe there are many angels in Wall Street," said Gilbert, in the same tone of good-humor.

"No more of your impudence!" said Moore, snappishly, feeling that Gilbert had the better of him in this little passage of words.

"What have I said that is impudent?" asked Gilbert, in astonishment.

"No matter. Go to your work."

"What a disagreeable fellow!" thought our hero. "I don't think I shall enjoy having him over me. He seems determined to find fault."

"Go over to Smith & Dixon's, and ask them for a Union Pacific First, on our account—stay; here's an order."

"All right, sir."

"And don't be gone all day."

"I shall be back as soon as I can," said Gilbert, coldly.

"Mind you do!" said Moore, in an aggravating manner.

It was a comfort to Gilbert that Mr. Moore did not venture to treat him in this way while Mr. Sands was in the office. Then, if he had occasion to speak, it was in a proper tone. But for two or three hours during the day the broker was absent at the Stock Exchange, and during this period the clerk saw fit to treat him with rudeness. This treatment, which commenced on the first day, was continued. Gilbert made little effort to conciliate Simon Moore (this was the clerk's full name), for he saw in advance that he would have small chance of succeeding. He was convinced of it when he discovered the relationship between Moore and his predecessor, and learned, moreover, that the clerk was a boarder in his cousin's family.

"I shall have to be very careful," thought Gilbert, "or Mr. Moore will get me into trouble of some kind. He wants to get rid of me, for some reason or other."

Gilbert came to the only sensible determination: to do his duty as well and faithfully as he knew how, and trust to Providence for the issue. He decided not to trouble himself too much about the clerk's enmity, since he knew that he had done nothing to deserve it.

At a little before four Gilbert left the office, and sought the counting-room of Mr. Briggs. He found that gentleman ready to go up-town.

"Well, Gilbert," he said, "how do you like your first day in business?"

"Very well, sir. I think I shall get on."

"Then you don't find your duties hard?"

"No, sir; they are pleasant and easy."

"You will find Mr. Sands very considerate and kind, I am sure."

"I like him already, sir."

"That is well," said Mr. Briggs, in a tone of satisfaction. "The next thing is to find you a boarding-place."

"Yes, sir. I shall be very glad to get settled."

"There will be little difficulty about that. If we start immediately, I can select a place for you this afternoon."

They took the street-cars at the Astor House.

"I have been thinking, Gilbert," said his guardian, "that Waverly Place or Clinton Place will be a good location for you. It is not so far but that on pleasant days you can walk to your place of business. This will save car-fare, which, though a small matter, is yet to be considered where your income is so small."

"How far is it, sir?"

"About two miles from Wall Street."

"I shan't mind that. When at school I used to walk ten miles sometimes, on holidays."

"Mind, Gilbert, I only recommend it. I will see that you have money enough to get along comfortably, even if you choose to ride constantly."

"I shall enjoy the walk when it is pleasant."

"Clinton Place is the western portion of Eighth Street," said Mr. Briggs. "East Eighth Street is known as St. Mark's Place. There are numerous boarding-houses there also, but I think you will like Clinton Place better. I suppose you are not very familiar with the streets yet?"

"No, sir; but I shall get accustomed to them as soon as possible. I found, this morning, that it is a useful thing to know."

About twenty minutes' ride brought the car to Clinton Place.

"We will get out here," said Mr. Briggs. "As we pass through the street," he said, "we shall probably notice papers pasted on some of the houses, indicating that boarders or lodgers will be received. At some of these houses we will inquire."

It was as Mr. Briggs had said. They had scarcely began their walk towards Broadway, when they saw such a paper on a neat-looking brick house.

"Let us inquire here, Gilbert," he said.

He went up the steps, and rang the bell. On a servant appearing, he announced his business. This brought about an interview with the landlady.

"Do you wish a room for two?" she asked.

"No; only for this boy."

"We have a hall bedroom on the third floor, and an attic room," said the landlady.

"We will look at the hall bedroom."

It was a small room, about seven feet by nine, and the furniture was very common.

"You can't expect anything very luxurious, Gilbert," said Mr. Briggs. "Shall you be contented with this room?"

"Yes, sir," answered Gilbert, promptly.

"What is your price, madam?" asked Mr. Briggs.

"With board, six dollars a week."

"I think we will try it," he said. "Will you stay here to-night, or come to-morrow, Gilbert?"

Gilbert thought of Mrs. Briggs, and answered, "I will begin now. I suppose I shall need to send for my trunk."

"I will send it by an expressman—to-night, if possible."

"In the case of strangers," said the landlady, hesitating, "we expect something in advance."

"I will pay you a week in advance," said Mr. Briggs.

He drew six dollars from his pocket-book, and handed it to the smiling landlady.

"Of course, sir," she said apologetically, "it isn't necessary with a gentleman like you, but it is our custom."

"Quite right, madam. I may as well tell you that I will be responsible for this boy's board. Here is my card."

Mr. Briggs was a well-known business man, and his name was familiar to the landlady.

"I am glad to have a friend of yours in my house," she said. "I hope the young gentleman will find everything satisfactory."

"I don't think he will be hard to please. Good-evening, madam. Good-night, Gilbert. You must call and see us often."

Mr. Briggs withdrew, and Gilbert sat down on the bed and tried to realize his new position. Less than a week had elapsed since he left school. Now he had entered on a business career in New York. It made him feel years older, but he did not shrink from his new responsibilities. He rather liked them.

CHAPTER X.

THE NEW BOARDING-HOUSE.

NOT long after Gilbert took possession of his room, the bell rang for dinner. As at most New York boarding-houses, the last meal of the day was dinner, not supper. Gilbert heard an adjoining door open, and, leaving his own room, followed the occupants down to the dining-room, which proved to be in the front basement.

The room was deep, and allowed of a long table, large enough for the accommodation of sixteen boarders. Mrs. White, the landlady, did not herself sit down to the table, but superintended the servants, who acted as waiters.

"Where shall I sit, Mrs. White?" asked Gilbert.

"You may sit here, between Mr. Ingalls and Miss Brintnall."

Neither of these persons had appeared, but Gilbert took the seat pointed out.

One by one the boarders entered, until the table was full. Gilbert looked about him with considerable curiosity. Mr. Ingalls proved to be a young man of twenty-five, who was employed in a wholesale stationery store in William Street. Miss Brintnall was an elderly-looking young lady, who was engaged as teacher in one of the public schools of the city. Her face was of a masculine type, and Gilbert was not surprised to hear that she was a strong advocate of woman's rights.

Just opposite were seated Mr. and Mrs. Theophilus Bower. He was clerk in a dry goods house, and had been but three months married. He was an inoffensive young man, with hair parted in the middle, who appeared to be very fond of his young wife, who wore long ringlets, and seemed quite a fitting match for her husband. Gilbert was rather amused by the manner in which they addressed each other.

"Theophilus, my love, may I pass you the salt?"

"Yes, my dear."

Occasionally, that is, as often as opportunity offered, they would press each other's hands under the table, the pressure being accompanied by a languishing look, which nearly upset the gravity of Mr. Ingalls, who, in his endeavors to suppress his merriment, once came so near choking that he had to leave the table.

On the other side of Mr. Ingalls sat an actor at one of the city theatres, with his wife. He seldom engaged in general conversation, but spoke in low tones to his wife. Whether this sprang from natural reserve, or from his mind being preoccupied with his business, opinion was divided; but the natural consequence was that he was unpopular.

There were several other boarders, who will be referred to in due time. Among them may be mentioned Alphonso Jones, a man of thirty, whose seedy attire would seem to indicate limited means, but who lost no opportunity of boasting of his aristocratic connections, and his intimacy with the best society.

Mr. Ingalls was the first to notice his young neighbor. Mrs. White had introduced Gilbert to his right and left hand neighbor, but left him to make acquaintance with the rest as he could.

"Have you been long in the city, Mr. Greyson?" he asked.

"No," said Gilbert, "but a few days."

"I suppose you are on business?"

"I am in a broker's office on Wall Street."

"And I am in a wholesale stationery store not far from Wall Street. If you have no better company, we might go down-town together in the morning."

"Thank you, I should like company."

"That is, if you walk; I never ride except on stormy days."

"Nor shall I. It's only two miles, I believe."

"Scarcely that; some think two miles a long walk. My brother from Boston, who was here for a while, complained a good deal of the long distances in New York. In Boston business men have much less distance to travel."

"I never was in Boston," said Gilbert. "Is it a pleasant city?"

"It is the 'Hub of the Universe,' you know; so Dr. Holmes calls it, at any rate. Yes, it is a pleasant city, but small, of course, compared with New York. How did you happen to come to this boarding-house?"

"I saw a notice outside that boarders would be taken."

"I hope you will like it."

"I hope so. I am not very difficult to suit."

"You have not been long in your place of business, I suppose."

"No; I went there only to-day. I have always been at school till now."

"Out of the city?"

"Yes, at Dr. Burton's Boarding School, at Westville."

"I have heard of it."

Then, lowering his voice, he said, "I see, Mr. Greyson, you are looking at the happy couple opposite."

"They seem very happy," said Gilbert, smiling.

"Oh, yes, they are wrapt up in each other. However, that is better than to quarrel all the time. Do you see that tall, thin man at the end of the table, and the lady at his side?"

"Yes."

"There isn't much love-making between them. They have a room adjoining mine, and I have the privilege of listening to some of their disputes."

"Who are they?"

"Major McDonald and his wife. He is Scotch, I believe. They married each other for their money, I hear, and then discovered that neither had any to speak of."

The conversation was interrupted by Miss Brintnall, who was expressing her views on woman's rights.

"In my opinion," she said, "man is a cruel and despotic tyrant. He monopolizes the good things of this life, and only throws an occasional crumb to poor, ill-used women. Women, for the same work, are paid less than half as much as men. Take myself, for example. I work just as hard as the principal of my school, yet he gets three dollars to my one. Now, I want to know where is the justice of that?"

"Perhaps," suggested Mr. Bower, "he has a wife and children to support. You haven't, you know, Miss Brintnall. Of course, you couldn't, you know," he added, with a simper.

"I might have a husband and children to support, I suppose," said Miss Brintnall, severely.

"If that is the case, Miss Brintnall," said Mr. Ingalls, humorously, "you ought to let us know, that we may not cherish vain hopes."

Miss Brintnall smiled; she generally did smile on Mr. Ingalls, who was a favorite of hers. Indeed, it was generally thought at the table that she would have had no objection to becoming Mrs. Ingalls, though the young man certainly had never given her any encouragement, save by such jocular remarks as the foregoing.

"You will have your joke, Mr. Ingalls," she said good-humoredly; "but to return to my argument. Is there any one present that can deny the correctness of my statement, that man is a tyrant?"

"I can," said little Mrs. Bower, indignantly. "My Theophilus isn't a tyrant, are you, dear?"

"I hope not, my love," he answered, pressing her hand under the table.

Mr. Ingalls came near swallowing a piece of meat the wrong way, and Miss Brintnall sniffed contemptuously.

"There may be exceptions," she said, "but they only prove the rule; even in your own case, Mrs. Bower, you may change your mind some years hence."

"I never shall, I am sure. Shall I, Theophilus, dear?"

"No, my love."

Here Mr. Ingalls squeezed Gilbert's hand under the table, with a comic look, which proved very trying to our hero's gravity.

Miss Brintnall received unexpected help from Mrs. McDonald.

"I agree with you entirely, Miss Brintnall," said that lady, "and I don't believe there are any exceptions. Men always try to domineer over women."

"My experience is the other way," said the major.

"Of course, I expected to hear you say so," said the lady, tossing her head.

"Men are very forbearing, in my opinion," proceeded the major.

"And very unselfish, I suppose," sneered his wife.

"That's where you hit the nail on the head, ma'am."

"I think," said Alphonso Jones, "it depends very much on social rank. I have the privilege of being intimately acquainted with some of our very highest families, and I can assure you that they are very harmonious. Among the lower orders, no doubt, men often act like brutes; but it is from lack of refinement. My friends, the Tiptops, who have their villa at Newport, never exchange a rude word. I think you are too sweeping in your remarks, Miss Brintnall."

"I have not the honor of knowing your grand friends, Mr. Jones," said Miss Brintnall, sarcastically; "but I contend that human nature is everywhere the same. Money and rank don't change it. I think it very likely that some of your Fifth Avenue grandees beat their wives."

"O Miss Brintnall!" exclaimed Mr. Bower and Mr. Jones in chorus.

"Yes, I do believe it. I won't take a word back."

"I don't believe your husband will ever beat you, Miss Brintnall," said Mr. Ingalls, slyly.

"I think not," said the teacher, decidedly. "I should allow him all the rights which he could fairly claim, but I would not let him infringe upon mine."

"I wouldn't marry her for a million dollars," whispered Mr. Bower to his wife.

"Isn't she horrid?" was the shuddering reply.

Here some one started a new topic of conversation, and Miss Brintnall subsided.

CHAPTER XI.

A NEW ARRANGEMENT.

ABOUT nine o'clock that evening Gilbert's trunk arrived. He received it with satisfaction, and unpacked it at once, putting a part of his clothing into the drawers of a small bureau, which, with the bedstead and one chair, took up about all the space in his contracted chamber.

Mr. Ingalls stepped in as he was unpacking.

"You haven't got much extra room," he said.

"No, I wish my room was larger," said Gilbert; "but it is as large as I can afford."

"My room is at least twice as large, but by sharing it with another I pay no more than you do."

"You are in luck; that is, if your room-mate is agreeable."

"We get along very well, but I expect to lose him in a week. He is to leave the city. If you would like to take his place, I shall be glad to have you."

"Will it increase my board?" asked Gilbert.

"How much do you pay now?"

"Six dollars."

"No; you would pay the same as my room-mate."

"Then I will accept your offer with thanks."

"I hope you won't have cause to repent it," said Mr. Ingalls. "If you do at any time I will let you off."

"If you should marry Miss Brintnall," suggested Gilbert, with a smile, "you will have to give me warning."

"No Miss Brintnall for me!" said Ingalls. "I don't want to be a henpecked husband, or marry one who would insist on wearing the breeches."

"The lady seems partial to you."

"She is not only partial, but martial," said the young man, who was apt to indulge in poor jokes; "I would as soon marry an Amazon. When you get through unpacking, come to my room; you may like to see it."

"I have unpacked as much as I intend to to-night. I will go with you now."

Mr. Ingalls' room was square in shape, and of very good dimensions; it was better furnished also than Gilbert's. It contained two single beds, side by side, a good closet, a sofa, a bureau, rocking-chair, and several ordinary chairs. Several fair engravings adorned the walls, and Gilbert felt that it would be decidedly pleasanter for him to share such a room as this with a pleasant companion, than to reign sole master of a hall bedroom.

"How do you like it?" asked Mr. Ingalls.

"Very much better than mine. I shall be glad to change."

"Then we will consider the arrangement decided upon. Can I offer you a cigarette?"

"No, thank you; I never smoke."

"That is where you are sensible; I only indulge myself occasionally."

They sat for half an hour and chatted. Gilbert was favorably impressed by his new friend, who, though ten years older than himself, proved a congenial companion. At ten o'clock he bade him good-night, and went to bed.

His bed was not particularly soft or luxurious, but he slept soundly, and awoke in the morning refreshed. He took an early breakfast, and walked down-town with Mr. Ingalls.

When Mr. Moore, the book-keeper, arrived, Gilbert was already at work.

"A new broom sweeps clean," sneered Moore, in an unpleasant tone.

"Do you mean me?" asked Gilbert.

"Yes; you are trying to make Mr. Sands think you a model."

"I hope he won't think that, for he will find out his mistake."

"He *will* find out his mistake," said Moore; "I predict that."

"I intend to do my work faithfully," said Gilbert; "there will be no mistake about that."

"I've heard boys talk that way before. They don't deceive me."

Just then Mr. Sands entered. He greeted Gilbert pleasantly.

"So you are on hand in good season. I like to see that."

"I shall try not to be late, sir."

"Where do you board?"

"In Waverly Place."

"That is convenient as regards distance. You may go to the Post Office for letters."

As Gilbert started for the Post Office, a boy about his own age came up and joined him.

"Are you Mr. Sands' new boy?" he asked.

"Yes," answered Gilbert.

"You've got my place, then. I used to be there."

"Did you? I am sorry to have interfered with you."

"You won't like it. He is very hard to get along with."

"He doesn't look like it."

"He discharged me for just nothing at all. That's what my cousin, the book-keeper, says."

"Is Mr. Moore your cousin?" asked Gilbert, who began now to understand the cause of his own unpopularity with that official.

"Yes; he lives at our house."

Gilbert said nothing, judging that it would be repeated.

"I hope you will get another place," he said, politely.

"I don't want another place. I want to be where my cousin is."

Gilbert felt rather awkward.

"That is natural," he said; "I am sorry you are disappointed, but, of course, I am glad to get a place. I have to shift for myself, and it is necessary I should be earning money."

"You won't stay long; old Sands will discharge you."

"I hope not. If I do my duty faithfully, I don't see why he should."

"That won't make any difference. Didn't I discharge my duty faithfully?"

Gilbert did not know, and expressed no opinion. Moreover, he thought he would not inquire, preferring to remain neutral. Besides, he doubted whether he could fully rely on the correctness of John's statements.

"I don't want to lose my place," he said; "but if I do, I hope you will get it back again."

"Suppose you resign in my favor," suggested John, in an insinuating manner.

"I would rather not," answered Gilbert, who felt that this request was decidedly cool.

"Just as I thought," muttered John.

"Mr. Sands would not thank me for meddling with what is not my business. If he chooses, at any time, to put you back and dismiss me, he'll do so without any request from me."

John did not vouchsafe an answer, but walked off sullenly.

Nothing of any importance occurred during the day, except that Gilbert found the book-keeper as disagreeable as ever. It seemed impossible to suit him. This Gilbert correctly attributed to his disappointment that his cousin had been superseded.

About the hour of closing, Gilbert was surprised at the entrance of Mr. Briggs.

"How are you getting on, Gilbert?" he inquired.

"Very well, thank you, sir."

"Do you think you shall like this place?"

"Yes, sir, I think so."

"And you don't regret leaving school?"

"Yes, sir, I do; but that can't be helped, and I don't trouble myself with thinking of it."

"You are right there; are you ready to go up town?"

"Yes, sir."

"Come along with me, then."

When they were in the street, Mr. Briggs said, "I will tell you in a few words what I mean to do for you, so that you can have a fair understanding about money matters. I shall pay your board, and out of your wages you will be able to buy your clothes and provide for your other expenses."

"But, Mr. Briggs," said Gilbert, "I shall be able to pay part of my board. I do not wish to be such a burden to you."

"Say no more about it," said his guardian, hastily, "I insist upon that arrangement."

"But, sir, I shall want sometime to repay you for the money you spend on me."

"When you are a rich man, I will permit you to do so. Till then, think nothing of it."

"I am at least very grateful to you for your kindness," said Gilbert.

For some reason Mr. Briggs seemed uncomfortable whenever Gilbert spoke of gratitude, and tried to drop the subject.

"Randolph spoke of calling to see you this evening," he said. "Shall you be at home?"

"Yes, sir, I shall be glad to have him come."

Gilbert was rather astonished at such a mark of attention on the part of the young aristocrat, but determined to treat him cordially, for his father's sake.

CHAPTER XII.

RANDOLPH'S CALL.

RANDOLPH had expressed to his father in the morning an intention of calling upon Gilbert. His motive was not interest in our hero's welfare, but curiosity to find out how he was situated, as indeed he freely acknowledged.

"I wouldn't call if I were you, Randolph," said his mother.

"Why not?" asked her husband.

"Gilbert will move in a different sphere," said Mrs. Briggs, loftily. "I do not wish my son to form intimacies beneath him."

"I don't intend to," said Randolph; "I want to see what sort of a place he is in."

"He will be likely to presume upon your condescension, and boast of you as one of his friends."

Mr. Briggs understood Gilbert better.

"No fear of that!" he said. "Gilbert is a boy of spirit. He is not one to seek or accept patronage. His pride is quite as great as Randolph's."

"What has he to be proud of, I should like to know," said Mrs. Briggs, with a sneer.

"He is my ward," said Mr. Briggs, stiffly, "and it is quite proper that my son should pay him some attention."

"You seem to be infatuated about that boy," said his wife coldly. "I suppose you will want him invited to Randolph's birthday party next month."

"I certainly shall," said Mr. Briggs.

"This is going rather too far," said his wife angrily.

"However that may be, he must be invited."

"I should think I had some voice in that matter, Mr. Briggs."

"Unless Gilbert Greyson is invited, there shall be no party at all," said Mr. Briggs, with decision.

Mrs. Briggs felt that the fiat had gone forth. Her husband generally yielded to her, but sometimes he put his foot down, as the saying is, and was not to be moved. She felt very much annoyed, but Randolph offered her a way of yielding gracefully.

"Oh, let the beggar come," he said. "He will be good fun. I want to see how he will behave."

"Since you wish it, Randolph," said Mrs. Briggs, addressing herself pointedly to her son, "I will make no further objection. It is your party, and you ought to have your own way. But I shouldn't think it was necessary for you to call on the boy. He is at some cheap boarding-house, I suppose."

"Cheap, but perfectly respectable," said Mr. Briggs.

"I want to see what a cheap boarding-house is like," said Randolph; and his mother said no more.

At eight o'clock the servant brought up to Gilbert's room a card bearing the name of Randolph Briggs.

"It's a young gentleman that wants to see you," she explained.

"I will go down and bring him up," said Gilbert.

He hurried downstairs, and found Randolph waiting in the parlor.

"I am glad to see you, Randolph," he said cordially; "will you stay here, or come up to my room?"

"I would like to see your room," said Randolph.

"It isn't much to see," said Gilbert; "but I shall be glad to have you come up."

"It's a long way down-town," said Randolph.

"All the better for me. I am nearer my place of business."

Gilbert's room was on the third floor, back. He opened the door and invited Randolph in.

"What a small place!" exclaimed Randolph, looking around him.

"So it is," said Gilbert; "but I make it do."

"And the furniture is extremely common," remarked his visitor, critically.

"That is true also," said Gilbert, laughing.

"There does not seem to be much of it either; you have but one chair."

"Take that, if you please, and I will sit on the bed."

Randolph sat down, but not till he had examined the chair carefully to see if it was clean.

"I don't see how you can live in such a place," remarked the young aristocrat.

"Oh, I easily accommodate myself to it," said Gilbert; "but I hope soon to make a change for the better."

"Indeed!"

"Yes; a young man in the house has a large room, which he has agreed to share with me as soon as his present room-mate leaves. That will probably be in a week. Then I can offer you a better reception."

"What is the young man's name?"

"Ingalls. I believe he comes from Massachusetts."

"Is he in business?"

"Yes; he is in a stationery store on William Street. Of course, he is a new acquaintance, but I think we shall get on well together."

"What sort of boarders have you here?" asked Randolph, curiously.

"Rather a miscellaneous class. The gentlemen are chiefly in business. There is one public school-teacher—a lady."

"Of course, there is nobody that moves in good society?"

"I really don't know."

"How much board do you pay?"

"Six dollars."

"Six dollars!" repeated Randolph, turning up his nose.

"Some of the boarders pay considerably more, but my room, as you see, is small, and that makes it low for me."

"What sort of a table have you?"

"Plain, but as good as could be expected. Of course it don't compare with yours."

"I should say not."

"But I find no fault with it. Everything is served neatly, and that is what I care most about."

At this point Mr. Ingalls knocked at the door.

"Excuse me," he said, when he saw Randolph; "I didn't know you had company."

"Come in," said Gilbert; "or rather, if your room-mate is out, let us adjourn to your room. We shall be more comfortable."

"Certainly; I shall be glad to have you."

"Mr. Randolph Briggs, Mr. Ingalls," said Gilbert, by way of introduction.

"I am glad to make your acquaintance, Mr. Briggs," said the young man.

Randolph bowed condescendingly.

They went at once to the larger room.

"This is much better," said Randolph, who seemed surprised to see a sofa.

"Yes, I shall consider myself promoted when I get here."

"Are you in business, Mr. Briggs?" asked Mr. Ingalls.

"Oh, no, I am preparing for college," said Randolph; "there is no need of my going into business."

"I wish I could have gone to college," said Gilbert, regretfully.

"It takes money to go to college," said Randolph, complacently; "I intend to live in style when I go there."

"I am afraid, Gilbert," said young Ingalls, "we must put off going till our wages are raised."

"I must put it off forever," said Gilbert.

"I have hopes of getting ready when I am fifty," said the young man; "perhaps Mr. Briggs will be a professor at that time."

"I wouldn't teach," said Randolph, "though it is very respectable to be a professor. I shall be a man of fortune."

Mr. Ingalls glanced quietly at Gilbert. He was evidently amused by the self-importance of the young aristocrat.

"Do you like your place, Gilbert?" asked Randolph.

"Pretty well."

"You haven't got any ice-water here, have you?"

"I will go down and order some."

While Gilbert was gone, Randolph said, "I am glad Gilbert has got a place, for he is poor and needs it. My father has done a great deal for him; but then he can afford it, for he is a rich man. I have no friends in this neighborhood; but I thought I would come down to see how he was getting along."

"Gilbert ought to be very grateful," said Mr. Ingalls, dryly.

"I think so, too. It is not every poor boy who has a rich man to help him."

Here Gilbert re-entered with the water, and shortly after Randolph left.

"What do you think of him, Mr. Ingalls?" asked Gilbert.

"He seems to think a good deal of himself," said the young man. "He referred to you in a very patronizing way."

Gilbert laughed.

"His mother has spoiled him," he said; "she is the most disagreeable woman I ever saw. If Randolph had been brought up differently, he might not show so much foolish pride. I like his father best of the three."

Gilbert little suspected that the man whom he praised had been, thus far in life, his worst enemy.

CHAPTER XIII.

GILBERT CALLS ON THE VIVIANS.

AS the boarders rose from the dinner-table on Friday, Alphonso Jones addressed Gilbert.

"Let us take a walk," he proposed.

"Thank you," said Gilbert; "but I have an engagement."

"I suppose there is a lady in the case," said Alphonso, slyly.

"There is a young lady where I am going," answered Gilbert.

"So I thought. I suppose you wouldn't be willing to mention names?"

"Oh, yes. I am going to call on Mr. Vivian, in West Forty-eighth Street."

"What! Mr. Vivian, the great merchant?" asked Jones, surprised.

"I believe he is an extensive importer."

"That's the one I mean. How in the world did you get acquainted there?"

"I haven't been long acquainted," said our hero.

Alphonso Jones was a young man who, in England, would be called a tuft-hunter. He aspired to be on visiting terms in families of high social position; but thus far had not met with much success. This did not prevent him from boasting continually of intimacy in quarters where he was not even acquainted. He did not dream that his little imposture was easily seen through by most of those who knew him, but was complacent in the thought that he was classed with that aristocracy, which he admired from a distance.

"Don't you know the Vivians, Mr. Jones?" asked Mr. Ingalls. "I thought you knew everybody that was worth knowing."

"So I do," said Alphonso, with an air of importance,—"that is, nearly everybody. I met the Vivians, I believe, at Saratoga, but did not have a chance to cultivate their acquaintance. Greyson, will you do me a favor?"

"What is it?" asked Gilbert.

"Let me accompany you this evening to Mr. Vivian's. You can introduce me as your friend, in case they do not remember our former meeting."

"I should like to oblige you, Mr. Jones," said Gilbert, "but my own acquaintance is too limited to allow me to take such a liberty."

"Just as you say, of course," said Alphonso, crestfallen. "I dare say I shall soon meet them at some fashionable party."

"So it will really not make much difference," suggested Ingalls.

"Oh, very little," said Mr. Jones, nonchalantly. "I thought perhaps Mr. Greyson might like the company of one who was used to society. I think, on the whole, I will call on my friends, the Montmorencys, this evening."

"Where do they live, Mr. Jones?" asked Mr. Ingalls.

"They occupy an elegant mansion on Fifth Avenue," answered Alphonso, consequentially.

"Couldn't you take me along with you?" asked Mr. Ingalls, demurely.

"I fear not," said Alphonso. "The fact is, Mr. Ingalls, the Montmorencys are very exclusive, and have expressly said to me more than once, 'We are always glad to have you drop in, Mr. Jones, for we look upon you as one of ourselves; but bring no strangers. Our circle is already extensive, and we cannot add to it.' Very sorry, of course."

"So am I, Mr. Jones," said Mr. Ingalls. "I should like to know a few high-toned people. How fortunate you are in knowing so many! What is the number of the Montmorencys' house?"

"I always forget numbers," said Alphonso, rather confused (for the whole story of the Montmorencys was a fiction), "but, of course, the house is familiar to me. It's on Murray Hill."

"That fellow is a humbug, Gilbert," said Ingalls, as he and his room-mate entered their own apartment. "He pretends to have a great many fashionable friends; but it's all a sham. Some day I'm going to teach him a lesson."

"How?"

"Introduce a friend of mine, a good amateur actor, as a French count. Fancy his delight at making each an aristocratic acquaintance!"

"Let me know when the time comes," said Gilbert, laughing.

"You shall assist me in it. I hope you will have a pleasant call this evening."

"I have no doubt of it."

Gilbert dressed himself carefully, and at half-past seven started on his visit. The evening was pleasant, and he decided to walk. Just opposite the Hoffman House he fell in with Randolph Briggs.

"Hallo, Gilbert," called out Randolph, "where are you bound,—to our house? I don't believe you'll find anybody at home."

"I am bound elsewhere," said Gilbert

"Where?" asked Randolph, curiously.

"To Mr. Vivian's."

"To call upon Laura?"

"My call will not be exclusively upon her," said Gilbert.

"Take my advice and don't go," said Randolph actuated by jealousy.

"Why not?" Gilbert asked, quietly.

"They might look upon it as an intrusion."

"I don't think they will, as I was specially invited for this evening."

"Out of politeness. Probably they have forgotten all about it."

"It appears to me, Randolph, that you take a good deal of interest in this matter," said Gilbert, amused.

"Oh, I care nothing about it; only as a friend I thought I would just mention that it might be thought rather presumptuous to take advantage of the accident that made you acquainted with Laura, to force yourself upon the family. If I were a poor boy like you, I would be careful to associate with my own class."

Gilbert was provoked at Randolph's insolence, as he rightly considered it, and answered coldly, "I will think of your advice, Mr. Briggs. I appreciate your motives in offering it."

"What does he mean?" thought Randolph, following with his eyes his father's ward. "I believe the fellow is angry with me. Poor and proud, I dare say. The Vivians will soon get tired of him."

But though he tried to console himself with this reflection, it chafed Randolph not a little that Gilbert should be invited to a house which he could not hope to enter.

Gilbert kept on his way to Mr. Vivian's house arriving about eight o'clock.

"Is Mr. Vivian at home?" he inquired of the servant who answered his summons.

"He went out for half an hour; will you come in and wait for him?"

"Is Miss Laura in?"

"I believe she is."

"Then you may hand her my card, if you please."

Gilbert was ushered into the parlor. He did not have to wait long. Laura entered and cordially offered her hand.

"I am very glad to see you, Gilbert—Mr. Greyson, I mean."

"Never mind about Mr. Greyson," said Gilbert, smiling. "Call me Gilbert, if you don't mind."

"Then I will," said Laura, frankly. "Do you know, I already begin to look upon you as an old friend."

"I am very glad of that, Miss Laura."

"My father went out for half an hour, as the servant probably told you. He bade me keep you till his return."

"Thank you; I shall be very glad to stay."

"I met a friend of yours on Fifth Avenue yesterday, Gilbert."

"Who was it?"

"Randolph Briggs."

Gilbert smiled.

"I don't know how far he is my friend," he said; "though he told me this evening he was, and as a friend he ventured to give me some advice."

"Indeed?" said Laura, looking the curiosity she felt.

"Would you like to hear what it was?"

"I certainly should, for it doesn't strike me that Randolph Briggs is particularly qualified to give advice to anybody."

"He advised me not to come here."

"Not to come here! Why not?" exclaimed Laura, impetuously.

"He said I was only invited out of compliment, and that my visit would probably be considered an intrusion."

"I wonder how he dared to say such things!" said Laura, indignantly. "What can he know of our feelings? Why, he isn't on visiting terms here himself!"

"I suppose he meant it for my good," said Gilbert.

"I am glad you didn't take his advice, Gilbert."

"I didn't care to deprive myself of a pleasure. Besides, I thought I could soon judge for myself whether you looked upon me as an intruder."

"What do you think about it?" asked Laura. "You have been here long enough to decide."

"I think I will stay a little longer."

Just then a boy of ten opened the door of the parlor.

"Laura," he said, "mother wants you to bring Mr. Greyson into the library."

CHAPTER XIV.

A PLEASANT EVENING.

GILBERT was presented to a pleasant-looking lady, whom Laura introduced as her mother.

"I am glad to see you, Mr. Greyson," she said, cordially; "I supposed Laura would bring you in here at once, but it seemed to be her intention to monopolize you."

"We had important business to talk over, mamma."

"Very important, no doubt. How do you like the city, Mr. Greyson?"

"I think I shall like it after I am better acquainted," Gilbert answered.

"You haven't introduced me, Laura," said her brother Fred, in an aggrieved tone.

"Gilbert," said Laura, "let me introduce to your favorable notice my brother Fred, who, in his own opinion, is a model of all the virtues."

"I am glad to meet him. I never saw a model boy before," said Gilbert, pleasantly.

"I never pretended to be a model boy," said Fred. "Laura's only chaffing."

"Where did you pick up that word, Fred?" said his mother.

"Isn't it a good word, mamma? It's just what she does."

"Fred has just commenced Latin," said Laura, "but I am afraid, from his own story, that it is just wearing out his constitution."

"I don't see any good in it," said Fred. "Do you know Latin, Mr. Greyson?"

"I have studied it some."

"How far have you been?"

"I have read Cæsar and Virgil."

"Oh, then you know a lot about it. I'm only in the second declension."

"You don't like it, then?"

"Not much. I don't see how anybody could ever talk such stuff."

"You will be more interested in it as you get on further. That was the way with me. I wasn't in love with it at first."

"I hope so," said Fred.

Here Mr. Vivian entered, and greeted Gilbert cordially.

"I told Laura to keep you," he said. "What have you been doing since we met?"

"I have got a place, or rather Mr. Briggs got one for me."

"What sort of a place?"

"I am with Mr. Sands, a stock-broker. His office is on Wall Street."

"I know of him, though I don't personally know him. How do you like your new situation?"

"I have not been there long enough to decide. I like Mr. Sands."

"Are you still an inmate of Mr. Briggs' house?"

"No, sir; I am boarding on Clinton Place, near Broadway."

"You find that more convenient to your office?"

"Yes, sir."

"Then you have fairly got started in your business career. I hope you may be successful."

"Thank you, sir."

"I believe you told me that your money, of which Mr. Briggs had charge, has been entirely expended on your education?"

"Yes, sir."

"Are you compelled, then, to live on your weekly wages?"

"I don't think I could do that very well, as they only amount to five dollars a week. Mr. Briggs offered to pay my board, and let me use this for other expenses. I don't like to have him do it, but he insists upon it."

"That seems kind," said Mr. Vivian. "Was it your idea, or his, to go to a boarding-house?"

"I suspect," said Gilbert, hesitating, for he was not clear whether he ought to tell this, "that it was Mrs. Briggs' idea. From the first, she has not seemed to like me."

"I don't like her looks," said Laura; "I have seen her several times. You know, papa, she was at the same hotel with us at Saratoga. She looks cross."

"You must not speak too hastily against people, Laura," said Mrs. Vivian.

"I suspect Laura only shares the general feeling," said Mr. Vivian. "Mrs. Briggs is, by no means, a favorite in society."

"Nor Randolph, either," added Laura.

"I thought he was a beau of yours, Laura," said her father, slyly.

"He never was, papa. I used to meet him at dancing-school, and I have danced with him there; but that is the end of our acquaintance. If he bows to me I bow back, but I don't care to know any more of him."

"Can't we have a little music, Laura?" asked her father.

"I only play a little. Do you play, Gilbert?"

"No, Miss Laura."

"Or sing?"

"A little."

"Then I'll make a bargain; I will play if you will sing."

"I hardly feel prepared to sing in company."

"This isn't company. You needn't mind any of us. Fred, open the folding-doors, will you?"

The piano was in the parlor adjoining. The doors were thrown open, and Laura sat down to the piano. Two or three songs were selected, and Gilbert sang to Laura's accompaniment. He had a good voice, and a correct ear, and the double performance passed off smoothly.

"Doesn't your brother sing?" asked Gilbert.

"Fred? He don't know one tune from another; besides, he don't like the piano. The hand-organ is his favorite instrument."

"I mean to buy one when I am rich enough," said Fred.

"Shall you go around with it?" asked Laura; "or only keep it in the parlor for the entertainment of visitors?"

"You may laugh as much as you like," said Fred; "but a hand-organ, that is, a good one, sounds splendid."

"Did you ever see such a barbarian? Gilbert, what else do you sing?"

The evening slipped away almost before they were aware. To Gilbert, it was positively delightful. Not that he was in love with Laura, but, never having had a sister, it was an agreeable novelty to him to meet a young girl so frank and attractive as Laura.

"I hope you will come again soon, Mr. Greyson," said Mrs. Vivian, when our hero rose to take his leave.

"Yes, do come," said Laura.

"I shall consider it a privilege to call," said Gilbert, with sincerity.

"By the way," said Mr. Vivian, "I have taken several tickets for a concert in Steinway Hall next Wednesday evening. I have a spare one for you, Mr. Greyson, if you have no engagement."

"I shall be very glad to accept one, sir."

"Then come up to dinner that evening; we dine at six. We will all go together."

"Am I to go?" asked Fred.

"There will be a ticket for you, if you would like to go, though I am afraid you won't enjoy the classical music you will hear."

"No matter," said Fred, "I'll go, though I'd rather go to a circus."

"If there were only a hand-organ, Fred would enjoy it," suggested Laura.

"Well, Gilbert, what sort of a time did you have?" asked Mr. Ingalls, when his room-mate returned.

"Delightful! I am going to dine there next Wednesday."

"It seems to me you are making a favorable impression in that quarter."

"I hope so."

A knock was heard at the door.

"Come in," said Mr. Ingalls.

Mr. Alphonso Jones opened the door and entered.

"Excuse my late intrusion, gents," he said. "And how did you find the Vivians, Mr. Greyson?"

"Very well, thank you."

"They are very high-toned people."

"I presume so, but I am not much of a judge," said Gilbert

"Probably," said Mr. Ingalls, "you do not know as many of that class as Mr. Jones. Did you find the Montmorencys well, Mr. Jones?"

"Quite so, thank you. Mrs. Montmorency has had a bad cold; but she has quite recovered now. They talk of going to Europe next summer."

"Do they, indeed? How you will miss them!"

"To be sure. However, I have many other friends in the first circles whom I can visit. I suppose, Mr. Greyson, the Vivians have a fine house?"

"It seems very comfortable."

"The Montmorencys live in a perfect palace. I wish you could see it."

"I wish I could, Mr. Jones," said Mr. Ingalls; "but you wouldn't take me, you know."

"I couldn't, Mr. Ingalls, as I explained to you. They are so very exclusive."

"I wonder visiting such fine houses doesn't make you dissatisfied with your own home."

"Oh, my tastes are very plain," said Alphonso.

"'Mid pleasures and palaces though I may roam,

Be it ever so humble, there's no place like home.'"

"Some of your own poetry, Mr. Jones?" asked Mr. Ingalls, demurely.

"No, it's Shakespeare or Byron," answered Jones; "I forget which. Good-evening, gents."

"Would you like to know where Mr. Jones spent the evening, Gilbert?" asked his room-mate.

"On Fifth Avenue?"

"No. Mr. Tarbox followed him, and saw him enter a billiard-saloon on the Bowery. Jones is a first-class humbug."

CHAPTER XV.

AT STEINWAY HALL.

SIMON MOORE, the book-keeper in the broker's office where Gilbert was employed, was a young man, somewhat under thirty. He understood his business very well, and thus far had given satisfaction to Mr. Sands. Personally, however, he was not agreeable. He was irritable and exacting, and had not been liked even by his cousin John, when the latter was office boy. Now, however, that John had been discharged, the book-keeper, as we have seen, made common cause with him, and John came to look upon him as a friend.

In this Moore was not altogether disinterested. John's mother, who was his aunt, kept a boarding-house, and found it difficult to meet her expenses. John's wages, though small, were important to her, and now that she was deprived of this resource, her nephew feared that he might be called on for assistance. It was in order to save his own purse that he desired to reinstate John in his old place. The readiest method that occurred to him was to prejudice Mr. Sands against Gilbert.

"Are you going out this evening, cousin Simon?" asked John, one evening.

"I may go out by and by."

"May I go with you?"

"If you want to."

Simon Moore was not always willing to be troubled with his cousin, but this evening he chanced to be in a pleasanter humor than usual.

"I have tickets to a concert, John," he said. "Would you like to go?"

"Very much," answered John, readily.

"The tickets were given me by a friend of mine, who is on the 'Times,'" explained Moore.

"Where is the concert, cousin Simon?"

"At Steinway Hall."

It was, in fact, the same concert to which Gilbert was invited by Mr. Vivian.

The book-keeper was not remarkable for his liberality, and John had been not a little surprised at receiving the invitation, until he learned that the tickets had cost his cousin nothing.

Eight o'clock found them in their seats at Steinway Hall. The concert did not commence punctually, and they had some time to look about them.

"Do you see any one you know, cousin Simon," asked John.

"Yes," said the book-keeper, "I see a particular friend of yours."

"A particular friend of mine!" repeated John, puzzled. "Where?"

"Five rows in front of this. There, near the centre of the hall."

"I don't see any body I know."

"It is Gilbert Greyson, your successor in our office."

"It is he, I declare. He is talking to a pretty girl beside him."

"That girl is the daughter of Mr. Vivian, the great importer."

"You don't say so. How on earth did he come to know her?"

"I can't say," answered Moore, coldly. "He is a very forward, pushing fellow. That may explain it."

"I hate him," said John.

"I don't love him overmuch myself," said Moore.

John and his cousin were not the only acquaintances who recognized Gilbert on that evening.

Randolph and his mother sat two rows behind the Vivians. Mr. Briggs had intended to come, but had a headache. He had suggested that the extra ticket be sent to Gilbert; but Mrs. Briggs had decisively objected.

"I don't care about having that boy seen with us in Steinway Hall," she said.

"Why not?" asked Mr. Briggs.

"I don't fancy him. Besides, he would be presuming on our kindness."

"I don't think he is the kind of boy to do that," said Mr. Briggs, who understood Gilbert much better than his wife. "It is a pity the ticket should not be used."

"If it were in a different part of the house, away from our seats, I should not care particularly," said Mrs. Briggs. "If he went with us, he might be thought to be a near relative."

"I don't think he would do us any discredit, either in appearance or in manners," said her husband.

"You are simply infatuated with that boy, Mr. Briggs. I am sure Randolph doesn't want his company."

"No, I don't," said Randolph.

"Like mother, like son," thought Mr. Briggs; but for the sake of peace he did not think it best to press the matter.

Soon after Randolph and his mother took their seats, the former discovered Gilbert sitting nearly in front of him.

"He's here, after all, mother," he exclaimed, in a low voice.

"Who is here, Randolph?"

"Gilbert Greyson. Don't you see him?"

"He's with the Vivians, too!" ejaculated Mrs. Briggs, unpleasantly surprised. "That boy doesn't appear to have a particle of shame."

"He needn't be ashamed of his company. I wish I were in his place."

"I don't mean that. He probably hinted to Mr. Vivian to take him, and he couldn't very well refuse."

"Very likely," said Randolph. "He's got plenty of cheek."

Both mother and son could see that Gilbert and Laura Vivian were conversing pleasantly, judging from the smiles on the faces of each.

"Mr. and Mrs. Vivian are not very wise in permitting such an intimacy between their daughter and a penniless boy," said Mrs. Briggs, frowning. "Some people are very unwise."

"I dare say he pretends he is rich, and boasts of father's being his guardian," suggested Randolph.

"I dare say you are correct," said Mrs. Briggs. "If I knew Mrs. Vivian, I would correct that wrong impression."

Here the music commenced, and the two were silent.

Randolph cared very little for the music, which was too classical to suit his taste. He did not expect to like it, but he went because he knew that the audience would be a fashionable one, and he liked to be seen on such occasions. Gilbert had more musical taste, and appreciated the greater part of what he had heard.

When the concert was over, he thanked Mr. Vivian cordially for the invitation.

"I have had a very pleasant evening, thanks to you, sir," he said.

"I am glad you have enjoyed it," said Mr. Vivian, kindly. "Come and see us soon."

"Thank you, sir."

Just after this parting, Gilbert fell in with Mrs. Briggs and Randolph.

"Good-evening, Mrs. Briggs," he said, politely. "Good-evening, Randolph. Where were you sitting? I did not see you."

"We saw you," said Randolph. "You were nearly in front of us."

"Did Mr. Vivian invite you to come?" asked Mrs. Briggs, coldly.

"Yes, madam."

"You are making the most of your chance meeting with them."

There was something unpleasant in her tone, and Gilbert detected it.

"They have been very kind and polite to me," he answered, in a reserved tone.

"I would not advise you to presume upon it too far," continued Mrs. Briggs.

"I don't intend to, madam," said Gilbert, stiffly. "I don't think I have."

"You seemed very attentive to Laura," said Randolph, with a characteristic sneer.

"It was my duty to be polite," said Gilbert.

By this time they had reached the street, and Gilbert said "Good-evening."

Neither Mrs. Briggs nor Randolph invited him to call, though the fact that Mr. Briggs was still his guardian would have made such an invitation only an act of ordinary politeness.

As he made his way toward Fourth Avenue, Gilbert brushed against Simon Moore and John; but having his mind occupied, he did not notice them.

"There he goes!" said John, enviously. "I wish I had as much cheek as that fellow has."

"You've got a fair amount, John," said his cousin, drily.

"I didn't know it," said John, aggrieved.

"Never mind, John," said the book-keeper, with unwonted good-humor. "Suppose we go in somewhere and have oysters. I feel hungry."

"So do I," said John, briskly. "I know a bully place near by."

"If it's a good place, you can lead me there. While we are discussing the oysters, I have a little plan to tell you about, that may give you back your place at our office."

"Good!" said John. "You're a true friend, cousin Simon."

Ten minutes later they were sitting in a curtained compartment, in a saloon famous for the excellence of its oysters.

In the next compartment, two minutes previous, Mr. Sands, the broker, had taken his seat and given his order; but of this neither John nor his cousin had the slightest suspicion.

CHAPTER XVI.

A PLOT AGAINST GILBERT.

THE next day Mr. Sands received an unexpected summons to Washington. A brother, who was clerk in one of the departments, was seriously ill, and he was summoned to his bedside.

"How long shall you be absent, sir?" inquired Simon Moore.

"I cannot say; it will depend on how I find my brother. Keep me apprised of what is going on by letter, and, if necessary, by telegraph."

"Yes, sir," said Simon, cheerfully; "you may rely upon me."

"Where is Gilbert?"

"Gone to the post-office."

"I have sometimes thought, Mr. Moore, that you were prejudiced against the boy."

"I was at first, sir," said Moore; "but on the whole he seems faithful, and disposed to do his duty."

Mr. Sands smiled slightly, but this Mr. Moore did not observe.

"I think well of him myself," he said.

"If he does well, he won't have reason to complain of me," said the book-keeper.

Again Mr. Sands smiled, but said nothing. Just as he was leaving the office for the cars, Gilbert returned.

"I wish, Gilbert, you would accompany me to the Courtland Street Ferry," said his employer. "I am going to Washington this afternoon."

"Indeed, sir!"

"I am summoned to my brother's sick-bed."

"When did you hear of his sickness, sir?" asked Gilbert, in a sympathizing tone.

"A week since; but last evening I learned by a telegram that he is dangerously sick."

By this time they were on their way to the ferry.

"You may take my valise, Gilbert," said the broker, "if you are willing."

"Certainly, sir," said Gilbert, politely. "I hope you will find your brother better."

"I certainly hope so. He would be a great loss to his family. By the way, how are you getting on with Mr. Moore?"

"I hardly know, sir," said Gilbert. "I don't think he likes me."

"Have you done anything to offend him?"

"Not that I am aware of. I have always treated him with respect."

"That is right. If you get into any trouble with him while I am away, come to me after I return, and tell me all about it."

Gilbert looked surprised, but of course promised to do so.

"I shall try not to get into any disturbance," he said.

"I hope you won't, but I fancy you will," said his employer.

"I hope you don't think I am quarrelsome, Mr. Sands."

"No, that is not my reason. I will say no more at present, except to request you, if anything happens, to give me a truthful and detailed account of it when I return."

"Thank you, sir, I will," said Gilbert, who, though puzzled, felt that his employer was friendly towards him.

Gilbert waited till the boat started, and then returned to the office. He regretted Mr. Sands' absence, for something told him that Mr. Moore would make it very disagreeable for him while he was gone. Indeed, the book-keeper was not long in showing his state of feeling towards our hero. As Gilbert entered, he looked up sharply from his desk.

"So you are back at last?" he said unpleasantly.

"Yes, sir," answered Gilbert.

"I thought you intended to remain away all day."

"Mr. Sands desired me to go to the ferry with him."

"He didn't desire you to stop to play on the way home."

"Did you see me playing on the way home?" demanded Gilbert, provoked.

"How could I when I was at work in the office?"

"Has any one reported to you that I stopped to play?"

"No."

"Then why do you charge me with it?"

"Look here, young man, I advise you not to try any of your impudence on me!" said Simon Moore, who, knowing himself in the wrong, was all the more angry. "I tell you, once for all, that I won't stand it."

"I don't intend to be impudent, Mr. Moore; but I do expect decent treatment from you."

"You are showing your hand pretty quick, young man. No sooner does Mr. Sands leave the city than you begin to put on your airs. I shall take care to report your conduct to him."

"I have neither done nor said anything that I am ashamed to have reported to him."

"Shut up!" said Moore, sharply.

Gilbert saw that there was no use in prolonging the dispute, and quietly went about his duties. While he was absent on an errand, a little later, his predecessor, John, looked in the door, and, seeing his cousin alone, entered.

"Good-morning, cousin Simon," he said. "Where is Mr. Sands?"

"Gone to Washington."

"He has? How long will he be gone?"

"A week perhaps."

John's eyes sparkled.

"That's favorable for us, isn't it?" he said.

Simon Moore nodded significantly.

"You are right there," he said. "When he gets back, Gilbert Greyson won't be here."

"You'll do what we were talking about last evening?"

"Yes, I shall have plenty of chances while Sands is away."

"Can't you manage it to-day?"

"No, it would look suspicious; I don't want Mr. Sands to suspect anything."

"How soon, then?"

"Say day after to-morrow. In order to avert suspicion, I will in my letter of to-morrow speak a good word for Gilbert,—say he's doing better than I anticipated, or something of that sort. The next day the explosion will come."

"You'll bounce Gilbert?"

"Yes, I'll take that upon myself, and explain to Sands when he returns. Ten to one he won't interfere then."

"And you'll take me in Gilbert's place?"

"Yes, I'll do that, too. But you must do better than you did last time. The fact is, John, you were lazy and careless. I was sorry to have you go, as you are my cousin; but I couldn't blame Mr. Sands much."

"Oh, I'll turn over a new leaf, cousin Simon," said John, readily. "You shan't have anything to complain of."

"I hope not."

Here Gilbert returned from his errand, and the conversation necessarily closed.

Gilbert nodded politely to John, though he took no particular fancy to him.

"So the boss is away?" said John, sociably.

"Yes, he has been called away."

"I suppose you are glad of it?"

"Why should I be?"

"When the cat's away, the mice can play, you know."

"This mouse does not care about playing," said Gilbert, smiling.

"Gilbert is a model boy," said Simon Moore, with a sneer.

"I never set up for one," said John, in a tone of congratulation.

"I should say not," sneered the book-keeper, who could not abstain from criticising even his cousin, in whose favor he was intriguing to oust Gilbert from his position. "However, I'll say this for you, that you are not a hypocrite."

"And I never want to be," said John, virtuously.

Of course Gilbert understood that here was another hit at him; but he was discreet enough to understand that it would do him no good to notice it.

Presently John turned to go.

"Is there anything I can do for you, cousin Simon?" he asked.

"Not to-day," answered the book-keeper, significantly. "You can look round again in a day or two."

"All right."

As John left the office, a small boot-black approached him.

"Shine yer boots?" he asked.

"Get out of my way!" said John, crossly, at the same time lifting his foot and kicking the boy.

"What did you do that for?" said the boy, angrily.

"Because I pleased."

"Then take that;" and the knight of the brush swiftly touched John's cheek with the dirty brush, leaving a black mark upon his assailant's cheek.

John would have renewed the attack, but a chorus of laughter at his appearance drove him back into the office to wash off the black mark.

"I'll wring his neck when I get a chance," muttered John, angrily.

"He wouldn't have touched you, if you had let him alone," said Gilbert. "Why did you kick him?"

"Because I pleased. Mind your business, or I may kick you, too."

"You'd better not," said Gilbert, quietly.

CHAPTER XVII.

THE PLOT SUCCEEDS.

THE third day was rainy, and Gilbert wore a thin overcoat, which, on arriving at the office, he took off and hung up. At ten o'clock the rain ceased, and he did not feel the need of wearing it when sent out on errands.

About eleven o'clock John sauntered into the office.

"You may go round to the post-office, Gilbert," said the book-keeper.

"Very well, sir."

Gilbert put on his coat and went out.

"Isn't it about time, cousin Simon?" asked John, significantly.

"Yes," said Moore.

"How shall we manage?"

The book-keeper took from his pocket a ten-dollar bill, and handed it to John.

"That is Gilbert's coat," he said. "Put this bill into one of the pockets."

John obeyed.

"I guess that will fix him," he said, in a tone of satisfaction.

"I'll manage the rest," said the book-keeper. "Stay round here till Gilbert gets back, and we'll bring matters to a crisis."

Just as John was placing the bill in Gilbert's coat-pocket, the little boot-black mentioned at the close of the last chapter thrust his head into the doorway.

"Shine yer boots?" he asked.

"Clear out, you vagabond!" said the book-keeper, irritably.

Tom, for that was his name, looked inquisitively about him and retired. He saw that there was no chance for business. He recognized John as the one who had kicked him the day before.

"I wonder what he was putting into the coat," he thought; but dismissed the thought as not concerning him till afterwards.

"Did he notice what I was doing?" thought John, with momentary uneasiness. "But, of course, he wouldn't understand," he felt, with quick relief.

A few minutes elapsed, and Gilbert returned, bringing home the mail.

"All right!" said Moore, "wait a minute, and I shall want to send you out again."

"Oh, by the way, Gilbert," he said, after a moment's pause, "have you seen anything of a ten-dollar bill?—I laid one on the desk an hour ago, and now it has disappeared."

"I haven't seen it, sir."

"Won't you look on the floor? It may have dropped."

Gilbert searched, but of course unsuccessfully.

"That is strange," said the book-keeper. "I remember distinctly placing the bill on the desk; have you seen it, John?"

"No, cousin Simon."

"It is very mysterious," mused the book-keeper.

"I hope you don't suspect me of taking it, cousin Simon," said John, who had been instructed what to say.

"Of course not."

John began to turn his pockets inside out.

"I want you to search me," he said; "if you don't, you may think I took it, after all."

"I never thought of such a thing, John," said Simon Moore.

"I am sure Gilbert and I would prefer to be searched," persisted John, looking towards Gilbert as he spoke.

Gilbert colored, for it was not agreeable to him to fall under suspicion, but he answered quietly, "I am quite ready to be searched."

"I don't think it at all necessary," said Simon Moore; "but if you boys insist upon it, I will do it. It is certainly strange that the bill should have disappeared, and left no trace behind. Gilbert, will you search John, and then he shall search you."

"If you desire it, Mr. Moore," said Gilbert; "but I don't believe John took the bill, and I am sure I didn't."

Gilbert proceeded to search John, the latter assisting him. A jack-knife, a couple of keys, a handkerchief, and twenty-five cents in money were all that he found.

"I'm not very rich," said John, smiling. "I don't mind saying that the ten dollars would be very acceptable, but I haven't got it; are you satisfied?"

"Yes," said Gilbert, "you haven't got it, and I didn't think you had; you may search me now."

John conducted the search carelessly, for he knew, beforehand, what the result would be.

"I don't find it," he said. "Where can the bill be? Are you sure you didn't put it back into your own pocket, cousin Simon?"

"Quite sure. By the way, Gilbert, didn't you wear an overcoat?"

"Yes, sir; there it is, hanging up."

"John, you had better examine that also, that the search may be thorough."

"Certainly," said Gilbert, little dreaming of what was in store for him.

John plunged his hand into one pocket and found nothing; then into the other, and drew out the ten-dollar bill.

"What's this?" he asked, pretending to be surprised.

"Let me see it," said Gilbert, overcome with surprise.

"Let *me* see it," said Simon Moore, sharply.

"It's a ten-dollar bill," said John, looking at it more closely.

"It's the note I missed," said the book-keeper, taking it into his hands. "What have you to say to this, Greyson?" he demanded, sternly.

"I have this to say," said Gilbert, a little pale, as was natural, "that I don't know anything about that bill, or how it came in my coat-pocket."

"I suppose not," sneered the book-keeper.

"I am willing to swear to it," said Gilbert, recovering his firmness.

"A boy that steals money cannot expect to be believed, even upon oath," said the book-keeper.

"Do you believe I took that money, John?" asked Gilbert.

"You mustn't ask me," said John. "I didn't think you'd do such a thing, Gilbert, but it looks mighty suspicious."

"I never stole a penny in my life," said Gilbert, hotly.

"Do you claim this money as yours?" asked the book-keeper.

"No, I don't."

"Then how came it in your pocket? It couldn't have got there without hands."

A light dawned upon Gilbert's mind; a suspicion of the truth flashed upon him.

"It is true," he said, significantly. "Somebody must have put it into my pocket."

"And that somebody was yourself," said Moore, sharply.

"Of course it was," chimed in John.

Gilbert looked slowly from one to the other. There was something in their faces that revealed all to him.

"I think I understand," he said. "You two have formed a conspiracy to ruin me. I see it now."

"If you speak in that way again," said Moore, in a rage, "I will kick you out of the office."

"I should like to have you refer the matter to Mr. Sands," said Gilbert, betraying no alarm. "He will do me justice."

"I ought to refer the matter to the nearest policeman," said the book-keeper, in a menacing tone.

"Do so, if you like," said Gilbert, though he shrank with natural reluctance from being arrested, innocent as he knew himself to be. "I am not without powerful friends, as you will find."

"Don't have him arrested, cousin Simon," said John, with apparent compassion. "He has given up the money. Discharge him, and let him go."

This was what Simon Moore had already determined to do. He knew very well that in any legal investigation John and he would incur suspicion, and for prudential reasons he preferred not to court any such publicity.

"I ought to arrest you," he said, turning to Gilbert; "but I will have pity on your youth, hoping that this will be your last offence. I shall, of course, discharge you, since I should not be justified in retaining you under the circumstances. I will report to Mr. Sands why I was compelled to dispense with your services. I will pay you your wages up to to-day, and you need not come here again."

"Don't trouble yourself about that, Mr. Moore," said Gilbert, with dignity. "I shall report to Mr. Sands when he returns, and abide by his judgment."

"You had better not," said Moore. "I advise you for your own good. Mr. Sands will still have it in his power to arrest you; your best course will be to leave the city, and go to some place where you are not known."

"I shall remain in the city, and can be found, if wanted," said Gilbert, boldly. "The day will come, Mr. Moore, when my innocence will be known by all."

Moore shrugged his shoulders.

"I have heard such things before," he said. "You can go. John, I will employ you, temporarily, in Gilbert's place."

"I understand your object now, Mr. Moore," said Gilbert, looking significantly at John.

"Begone, or I will yet have you arrested," said the book-keeper, angrily.

Gilbert put on his coat and hat, and walked out of the office.

CHAPTER XVIII.

AN HUMBLE FRIEND.

JUST outside the office from which he had been discharged, Gilbert was accosted by Tom, the boot-black.

"Shine yer boots?"

Gilbert shook his head.

"Only five cents, mister,—that's half price."

"That's cheap enough," said Gilbert; "but I've just lost my place, and I cannot afford to pay even that."

"Been bounced?" asked Tom.

"Yes."

"What for?"

Gilbert hesitated. He did not like to admit that he had been suspected of dishonesty; still he was innocent, and had nothing to be ashamed of in the matter. He accordingly related what had happened.

Tom whistled.

"Did you say the money was found in your pocket?" he asked.

"In the pocket of my overcoat," he replied.

"And was your coat hanging up?"

"Yes."

"Then I know how the money got there."

"You know how the money got into my pocket!" repeated Gilbert, in surprise.

"Yes, the other boy put it there."

"What other boy,—the boy that's in the office?"

"Yes, his name is John."

"How did you happen to see him do it?" asked Gilbert, eagerly.

"I went to the door to see if the book-keeper didn't want a shine; just as I was looking in, I see that boy John go to a coat, and put a bill into the pocket. I thought it was his coat, and wondered what made him keep his money loose in that way. Did he say you put it there?"

"Yes."

"He wanted you bounced—that's what's the matter."

"You are right; he wanted the place himself, and now he's got it."

"Just you go back and tell the book-keeper all about it, and I'll stand by you," suggested Tom.

Gilbert shook his head.

"It won't do," he said. "John is Mr. Moore's cousin, and I feel sure they are both in the plot; they would say you were lying."

"Let 'em say it," said Tom. "I'll punch their heads if they do."

Gilbert smiled at the zeal of his humble friend. "I am afraid that would do neither of us any good," he said.

"Won't you do nothin', then?" asked Tom, disappointed. "Will you stay bounced?"

"Yes, till Mr. Sands comes back."

"Is he the boss?"

"Yes; he is now in Washington, and may not return for several days. When he comes back, I shall want you to tell him all you saw."

"I'll do it," said Tom.

"What is your name? Where can I find you if I want you?"

"I hang out at the Newsboys' Lodge. My name is Tom Connor."

"Thank you, Tom; I'm very glad I met you. Your testimony will be valuable to me. Don't say anything about it to anybody else at present. I want to surprise them."

"All right."

"I think I will have a shine, after all," said Gilbert, wishing to repay his new friend by a little patronage.

"I'll make your boots shine so you can see your face in 'em," said Tom, dropping on his knees, and proceeding to his task energetically.

"That will save me the expense of a looking-glass," said Gilbert.

"So it will," said Tom.

When the last was completed, Gilbert drew ten cents from his pocket, and extended it towards Tom, but to his surprise the bootblack did not offer to take it.

"Never mind," said he, "I don't want no pay."

"Why not? You have earned it," said Gilbert, wondering at the refusal.

"You're bounced, and aint got no money to spare. I'll wait till you've got your place again."

"You are very kind," said Gilbert, grateful for the considerate sympathy of his humble present; "but I am not so badly off as some, for I have no board to pay. You'd better take the money."

"I'll take five cents," said Tom; "that'll be enough. I'd rather work for you for nothin' than for that other feller for full price."

"You don't like him, then? Did he ever employ you?"

"He kicked me yesterday; but I got even with him," he added, in a tone of satisfaction.

"How did you get even with him?"

"I blacked his face for him," said Tom, brandishing the brush.

Gilbert laughed.

"He didn't fancy that, I suppose?"

"He had to go back and wash his face," said Tom, laughing at the recollection.

"Well, Tom, good-by," said Gilbert, preparing to go. "I'll hunt you up when Mr. Sands gets back."

"You'll find me round here somewheres; this is where I stand."

Gilbert walked away, feeling considerably more cheerful and hopeful than before his interview with Tom. Now he felt that he had at hand the means of his vindication, and his idleness would only be temporary. He was shocked at the meanness and wickedness of John and the book-keeper in forming such a conspiracy against him. He was already learning the lesson of distrust, and that is never a pleasant lesson for any of us. Fortunately, we need not distrust everybody. He must be indeed unfortunate who does not find some true friends to keep up his faith in humanity. Our hero had found one, who, though but a boot-black, was likely to be of essential service to him.

It is said that ill news travels fast. That very evening Mrs. Briggs learned that Gilbert had lost his situation, and from what cause. It happened in this way.

Randolph, chancing to be down-town, it occurred to him to call upon Gilbert. His call was made about half an hour after Gilbert had been discharged.

He entered the office, and, looking about, saw John, who appeared to be employed. He asked, in some surprise, "Does not Gilbert Greyson work here?"

"No," answered John promptly, "not now."

"How is that?"

"He was discharged this morning. Can I do anything for you?"

"Discharged!" exclaimed Randolph, much surprised. "What was he discharged for?"

Here Simon Moore took part in the conversation.

"Are you a friend of Gilbert Greyson?" he asked.

"Ye-es," answered Randolph, in a tone of hesitation. "That is, he's an acquaintance of mine."

"If you feel interested in him, I have unpleasant news for you."

Randolph pricked up his ears.

"What has happened?" he inquired.

"To be brief, I am afraid your friend is not strictly honest."

"You don't say so!" exclaimed Randolph, really amazed. "He hasn't run off with any money, has he?"

"He isn't very much interested in him," the book-keeper said to himself shrewdly. "He doesn't say anything in his defence."

"No; but I am afraid he would if the theft had not been detected so soon."

"What was it,—money?"

"A ten-dollar bill, which I laid casually on the desk, suddenly disappeared. It was found, after a little search, in the pocket of your friend's coat."

"He isn't my friend; he is only an acquaintance," said Randolph. "I don't know much about him. I didn't think he'd steal, though. Did he own up?"

"Not he; he was too brazen. Mr. Sands was absent from the city, but I did not hesitate to discharge him at once. In our business a boy must often be trusted with sums of value, and I should not feel safe in continuing to employ him."

GILBERT ACCUSED OF STEALING.

"I suppose you're right," said Randolph. "I wonder what father'll say."

"Well, I guess I'll be going," he continued. "I didn't expect to hear such news of Gilbert."

"We regret it very much," said the book-keeper, hypocritically.

"Of course," said Randolph. "Serves him right. He shouldn't have made such a fool of himself."

"That fellow don't care much about Gilbert, John," said Simon Moore, after Randolph's departure.

"That's so," said John.

"If he has no warmer friends than that, we shan't have any applications to take him back."

"I hope not," said John. "What do you think Mr. Sands will say when he finds me here?"

"If I tell him you have done your duty, and done all I required, he'll probably keep you. You must do better than you did last time. No fooling away your time in the streets when you are sent on an errand. It won't do."

"There won't be any trouble about me," said John, confidently.

CHAPTER XIX.

A DOMESTIC DISCUSSION.

RANDOLPH hurried home to tell his mother what he had heard about Gilbert's loss of employment. He knew well enough her feeling towards his father's ward to feel sure that it would be welcome intelligence.

"Detected in stealing money!" ejaculated Mrs. Briggs, triumphantly. "Just what I predicted all along. I am not often deceived about character."

"I never heard you predict it, mother," said Randolph.

"It was only because I did not like to speak against the boy," said Mrs. Briggs, only slightly discomfited. "I read it in his face the first day he came here. I saw he was sly and underhanded."

"Well, I didn't," said Randolph, who was less malignant than his mother. "I never thought he would do such a thing. I didn't like him, of course, but still I thought he was honest."

"I have lived longer in the world than you, Randolph," said Mrs. Briggs, sagaciously, "and I know that appearances are deceitful. I am not so easily taken in as your father. He has been infatuated about this disreputable boy. I hope the knowledge of the boy's baseness will cure him."

"I suppose we needn't invite Gilbert to my party, now?"

"No, of course not," said Mrs. Briggs, with emphasis. "It would be an insult to you to invite a boy convicted of theft."

"Father may insist upon it," said Randolph.

"Not unless he is bereft of his senses," said Mrs. Briggs. "He has made a point of it till now; but, of course, this will change his wishes."

Randolph did not reply; but, notwithstanding his mother's assurance, he felt some doubts on the subject. His father was, in general, yielding and easily managed; but, as is often the case with such men, he was, at times, unexpectedly firm.

This conversation took place just before dinner. It was interrupted by the arrival of Mr. Briggs, who went upstairs at once to prepare for dinner. Fifteen minutes later they met around the dinner-table. By arrangement with Randolph, Mrs. Briggs had reserved to herself the pleasure of imparting to her husband the news she had heard.

"I have heard some news to-day, Mr. Briggs," she commenced, in a premonitory tone.

"Indeed, my dear! Pleasant news, I hope."

"I don't think it will be pleasant to you, though, I must confess, it is only what I have all along anticipated."

"You speak in enigmas, Mrs. Briggs. Will you kindly be a little more explicit?"

"You are aware, Mr. Briggs, that I have always had a very unfavorable opinion of your protegé, the Greyson boy?"

"You certainly have not concealed your opinion of him," said her husband, shrugging his shoulders. "Yes, I may say that I know your opinion of him."

"I suppose you call it prejudice," continued the lady.

"Well, it certainly seems like it, not being founded on the knowledge of anything to his detriment."

"That was not necessary. There is such a thing as reading character. I judged him by his face."

"He seems to me to have a very frank, attractive face."

"As you read it," said his wife, contemptuously. "Well, this paragon of yours has lost his place."

"He has?" inquired Mr. Briggs, in evident surprise.

"Yes, he has, and I am not surprised to hear it."

"Do you know why he was discharged?"

"He was detected in theft—stealing a large sum of money!" answered Mrs. Briggs, triumphantly.

She expected that her husband would be overwhelmed at this disclosure; but he asked quite calmly, "How do you know this? Who is your informant?"

"Randolph."

"What do you know of this, Randolph?" asked his father.

Randolph gave his father an account of his visit to the office of Mr. Sands, and the information given him there.

"What do you say to that?" demanded Mrs. Briggs, in exultation. "Does that change your opinion of your paragon?"

"I think there is some mistake somewhere," said Mr. Briggs.

"Why should there be any mistake?" she asked. "Do you think Randolph would tell a lie?"

"There are other ways of accounting for the mistake. I have no idea that Gilbert is guilty of what is charged against him."

"Really, this is absurd. You are perfectly infatuated with this boy," said Mrs. Briggs, angrily.

"Mistakes have occurred before," said her husband, with provoking calmness. "I will investigate the matter."

"I don't see what investigation is needed. The boy has stolen the money. The book-keeper told Randolph so."

"The book-keeper may be mistaken."

"Not much chance of that."

"Or he may have taken the money himself and charged it upon Gilbert."

"Really, Mr. Briggs you are very perverse," said his wife, impatiently.

"Because I am not ready to believe Gilbert a thief before he is proved so."

"After he has been proved so."

"There would be no need of trials or juries if you were a judge, my dear," said Mr. Briggs, smiling. "You would be for sentencing the unfortunate defendant as soon as the charge had been brought against him."

"Cherish your delusion as to the boy's innocence as much as you like, Mr. Briggs; but there is one thing which you will certainly concede."

"What is that?"

"Gilbert Greyson must not be invited to Randolph's party."

"Why not?"

"A common thief—impossible!"

"But suppose he is wrongfully accused?"

"It is enough that he is accused, and probably guilty."

"I will investigate the matter, Mrs. Briggs. If I am convinced that the boy is innocent, he shall be invited."

Mrs. Briggs was about to make an indignant protest, when the servant, who had answered the door-bell, opened the door and ushered in the innocent cause of the heated discussion,—Gilbert Greyson.

CHAPTER XX.

A FEMALE FOE.

THERE was a moment of embarrassing silence after the entrance of Gilbert. Mrs. Briggs, as she afterwards expressed it, was paralyzed with astonishment at the effrontery of the boy. Randolph waited with curiosity to hear what his parents would say, while Mr. Briggs was silent merely because he was taken by surprise. He was the first to speak, and his tone, though a little embarrassed, was yet not without kindness.

"Good-evening, Gilbert," he said. "Won't you sit down and have some dinner?"

Mrs. Briggs looked daggers at her husband. How could he dream of extending such an invitation to Gilbert, under the circumstances.

"No, thank you," said Gilbert, "I have already dined."

"Then take a seat. We shall soon be through dinner."

"This is an unusual time to call," said Mrs. Briggs frigidly, breaking silence for the first time.

"What difference does it make?" interposed her husband. "Gilbert is not a stranger, to stand on ceremony."

"So it appears," returned his wife, in the same unpleasant tone.

"I ought to apologize for calling during your dinner-hour," said Gilbert, "but I wished particularly to consult you about my affairs."

Of course this was addressed to Mr. Briggs. Mrs. Briggs was perhaps the last person in the range of his acquaintance whom our hero would have cared to consult.

"Anything new with you?" asked his guardian, in a tone of slight embarrassment.

"Yes," answered Gilbert, frankly; "I am in trouble."

Mrs. Briggs glanced meaningly at Randolph, as if to say, "Now it's coming."

"You would perhaps wish to speak to me alone," said Mr. Briggs.

"Oh, if you have any secrets, Randolph and I can withdraw," said Mrs. Briggs, with unnecessary offence. She would have been deeply disappointed to be excluded from the conference between Gilbert and her husband. Our hero, however, relieved her of her apprehensions.

"Though I am in trouble," he said, "I have nothing to be ashamed of, and am perfectly willing to speak before all of you."

Mr. Briggs here glanced at his wife with a relieved air. Gilbert spoke as if confident of his own innocence. It produced no such effect on Mrs. Briggs.

"He's going to brazen it out," she said to herself.

"Go on, then," said Mr. Briggs, kindly. "What is your trouble?"

"I have been charged with theft, and dismissed from my situation," said Gilbert, candidly.

"Do you call that nothing to be ashamed of?" demanded Mrs. Briggs, sharply.

Gilbert met her hostile gaze with unflinching calmness.

"No," he said, "it is nothing for me to be ashamed of, for the charge is false."

"What evidence have we of that except your own assertion?" demanded Mrs. Briggs.

"That is enough for me," said Mr. Briggs.

"It is not enough for me," said his wife.

"I will give you an account of the affair so far as I understand it," said Gilbert. "Fortunately, I have a witness who is able to confirm my words."

Gilbert's statement need not be repeated, as the facts are already known to us.

"So you expect us to believe the testimony of this boot-black." said Mrs. Briggs, scornfully,—"a highly respectable witness indeed."

"I suppose a boot-black may speak the truth, madam," said Gilbert.

"I dare say he would say whatever he was instructed to say for twenty-five cents, perhaps less."

"You are determined to believe me guilty, Mrs. Briggs," said Gilbert, quietly, betraying no anger; "I expected it, for I knew you are prejudiced against me."

"I certainly don't believe the very extraordinary story you have told us," retorted the lady. "You charge a book-keeper, of high standing, with entering into a conspiracy against you. It is absurd upon its face."

"How do you know the book-keeper is of high standing?" asked Mr. Briggs.

"Because Mr. Sands would not have any other."

"Gilbert has the same guaranty of high standing," said her husband, smiling. "He has been employed by Mr. Sands."

"That is different. He took him upon your recommendation."

"Would I be likely to recommend any boy not of high standing?"

"Your levity seems to be ill-timed, Mr. Briggs," said his wife, coldly.

"I thought it my duty to come to you and tell you at once," said Gilbert.

"Knowing that you could not conceal it from us, for we knew it already," said Mrs. Briggs, who could not forbear another sneer.

"You knew it already!" exclaimed Gilbert, with unmistakable astonishment "Has Mr. Moore already sent you word of it?"

"No; Randolph happened to call at the office for you just after your discharge. He brought us the news."

"I am much obliged to Randolph for his call," said Gilbert; "I am only sorry that it occurred at such an unfortunate time."

"It was unfortunate for you, no doubt," said Mrs. Briggs.

"When I return there, I hope you will call again," said our hero, turning to Randolph.

Mrs. Briggs was exasperated by our hero's coolness.

"Have you the effrontery to fancy you will be taken back after such a crime?" she demanded.

"I have committed no crime, Mrs. Briggs. The charge is false, as I shall prove to Mr. Sands when he returns from Washington. He is a just man, and understands that the book-keeper is prejudiced against me."

"When will Mr. Sands return?" asked Mr. Briggs.

"In a few days. He has gone to the sick-bed of his brother. I shall wait till he returns before taking any steps to clear myself."

"It is probably your best course. I hope all will come out right."

"I think it will," said Gilbert. "Now, let me bid you good-evening."

"Why not stay the evening?" said Mr. Briggs, in a friendly tone.

"Thank you very much, but I will wait till I am cleared of this charge. I came up to-night because I wanted you to know about it."

"I will accompany you to the door," said Mr. Briggs.

When they were in the hall, he said, "Next Wednesday Randolph is to have a birthday party. I shall be glad to see you here."

"Thank you, sir," said Gilbert, gratefully. "I thank you all the more, because it shows that you believe in my innocence. But all the same, I would rather not accept. I shall still be resting under this false charge, and Mrs. Briggs evidently believes me guilty."

"Women are apt to be prejudiced," said Mr. Briggs, apologetically.

"Still the prejudice would make it unpleasant for me to come."

"Perhaps you are right, Gilbert. At any rate, you are manly and independent, and I respect you for it. Come round to my office if anything turns up in which you need my advice."

"Thank you, sir."

When Mr. Briggs returned to the dining-room, his wife accosted him.

"Well, you had a secret conference with your promising protegé," she said.

"Not secret. I am willing to tell you all that passed between us."

"Well?"

"I invited Gilbert to attend Randolph's party next Wednesday."

"Good heavens! Mr. Briggs," exclaimed the lady, angrily, "this is a little too much. Of course the boy snapped at it. He has more effrontery than any boy I ever knew."

"He declined the invitation," said Mr. Briggs. "He said that while resting under this charge he was unwilling to be present on such an occasion."

"Then he has more decency than I gave him credit for," said Mrs. Briggs, relieved. "Knowing his guilt, he would find it embarrassing."

"Permit me to differ with you, Mrs. Briggs. One thing more. I have only given Gilbert a verbal invitation. Let me request you to send him a personal invitation with the rest."

"What necessity is there for that? Has he not declined to come?"

"He must receive a formal invitation, nevertheless," said her husband, sternly, "or there shall be no party."

"Your father is so infatuated with that boy," said Mrs. Briggs, after her husband had left the room.

But she sent the invitation. She knew by her husband's tone that he was fully in earnest. She was still a little afraid that Gilbert would accept, and was only quite freed from apprehension when she received a note from him regretting that he could not be present.

CHAPTER XXI.

ALPHONSO JONES.

"WOULD you like a little fun this evening, Gilbert?" asked his room-mate, on the succeeding morning.

"Yes," said Gilbert; "I always enjoy fun, and especially now when I have lost my place, since it will help me to forget my bad luck. Is there anything up?"

"Yes; we are going to play a practical joke on Alphonso Jones. We are going to gratify his taste for associating with the aristocracy."

"What is your plan?"

"I have discovered in Bleecker Street a stylish barber, who has a smattering of French. In feet, he has served me more than once. He has entered into our plot, and agreed to personate a French count—the Count de Montmorency."

"Good!" said Gilbert, laughing. "When are the two to be brought together?"

"This very evening, in our room. I shall despatch a note to Mr. Jones during the day, inviting him to meet my illustrious visitor. Hayward and Kennedy are in the secret, and will be present also. Of course you will be with us, but you must keep on a straight face."

"Never fear for me," said Gilbert. "I will take care not to let the cat out of the bag."

In conformity with the plan, Mr. Alphonso Jones received, during the day, the following note:—

"DEAR MR. JONES,—I shall be glad if you will favor me with your company this evening, in my room. I have been fortunate enough to make the acquaintance of an illustrious French nobleman, Count Ernest de Montmorency, who, in the most condescending manner, has accepted an invitation to spend this evening with me. You will find him very affable and agreeable, notwithstanding his superiority in social rank. I feel a little diffident about receiving him, not being so well up in the usages of fashionable society as you are—I rely on you to help me out. I have invited Hayward and Kennedy also to be present. Greyson will, of course, be with us. If you have any other engagement, break it for my sake.

"Yours truly,

"W. INGALLS."

The face of Jones was overspread with smiles as he read this epistle, and he felt at least a foot taller. He could conceive of nothing more glorious than to be introduced to a foreign nobleman. Once in his life it had been his privilege to make the acquaintance of a brigadier-general, who had given him two fingers to shake, and said, "I am glad to meet you, sir." Most of the fashionable acquaintances of whom he boasted had no existence save in his imagination, but this general was a reality; he was only a general of volunteers, but that made no difference to Alphonso; he had managed hundreds of times to make capital of his greatness in some such way as this: "My friend, General Smith, remarked to me one day;" or, "Speaking of brave men reminds me of my intimate friend, General Smith." But even General Smith was not for a moment to be compared to the Count Ernest de Montmorency; there was something peculiarly high-toned in the name, Alphonso thought. So thought Mr. Ingalls, or he would have invented some other.

Alphonso was anxious to communicate to some one else the honor in store for him; he would like to have gone to his employer at once, and said, "Mr. Simpson, I am to meet the Count de Montmorency this evening." This, however, even to Alphonso, seemed rather an abrupt and uncalled-for announcement, and he had to consider how best to manage the matter, for he was determined that Mr. Simpson should know it. It was not entirely easy, but finally a bright and satisfactory idea dawned upon the happy Jones.

He went up to the desk, behind which his employer, a stout, practical man of business, was sitting, and coughed by the way of arresting his attention.

"Eh, Mr. Jones, did you wish to speak to me?" inquired Mr. Simpson.

"Yes, sir," said Alphonso; "would you be kind enough to let me leave the store half an hour earlier than usual?"

"If you have a good reason, Mr. Jones; are you sick?"

"No, sir, my health is excellent, thank you. The fact is, sir, I have an invitation to meet the noble count, Count Ernest de Montmorency, this evening, and—"

"The—what?" exclaimed his employer, arching his brows.

"A French nobleman, sir—the Count Ernest de Montmorency," repeated Alphonso, trying not to betray too strongly his inward exultation.

"What time are you going to meet him?"

"This evening, sir, but I wish time to dress properly."

"Well, I don't know that I have any objection," said the merchant, deliberately. "Where is this count stopping?"

"I don't know exactly, sir; but probably at the Brevoort House or the Clarendon."

"Very well, you can go. Business is not pressing, and you can be spared. But, hark you, Mr. Jones, one word of advice."

"Certainly, sir."

"If this count wants to borrow money of you, don't lend him."

"I am sure he wouldn't ask such a thing," said Alphonso, shocked at the idea. "Why, he possesses a beautiful chateau and an immense estate in France!"

Here Alphonso drew upon his imagination for what he considered to be probable enough.

"They all say so," said the practical Simpson, "even when they haven't twenty-five cents to bless themselves with. My advice may be needed, after all."

Alphonso was rather disgusted by this caution, which seemed so derogatory to the character and position of a nobleman; but he, after some reflection, attributed it to Mr. Simpson's disappointment in not himself enjoying the privilege of being invited to meet the count.

"Mr. Kidder," he said to a fellow-clerk, "what do you think of my necktie?"

"It looks well enough—why?"

"I was wondering whether it would do to wear this evening."

"What's up this evening?"

"I am invited to meet the Count Ernest de Montmorency, as you will see by this note."

"Strange Ingalls didn't invite me," said Kidder. "When did he pick up the count?"

"Really, Mr. Kidder, that is a singular way of speaking,—*picking up* the count," protested Alphonso.

"I have no great respect for French counts," said Kidder. "They don't generally amount to much."

"He's jealous, too," said Alphonso to himself, complacently. "It is clear he envies me my invitation."

"What do you think I ought to wear, Mr. Kidder?" he asked.

"Dress suit and white tie, of course."

"So I think. I'm really sorry I can't take you with me, Kidder."

"Oh, I couldn't go to-night. I've got a ticket to the theatre."

"I'd rather meet the count than go to forty theatres," thought Alphonso. "Wouldn't it be a splendid thing if he should take a fancy to me, and invite me to visit him at his chateau in *la belle France*?"

Alphonso made so many mistakes during the remainder of the day that he might have been spared considerably sooner without detriment to the business.

CHAPTER XXII.

COUNT ERNEST DE MONTMORENCY.

AT eight o'clock Alphonso knocked at the door of Mr. Ingalls' room. He was got up with the utmost magnificence which he could command. With his dress-coat, white tie, and imitation diamond pin, he made an imposing appearance.

"I am glad to see you, Mr. Jones," said Mr. Ingalls. "Count Ernest de Montmorency, permit me to introduce my friend, Mr. Alphonso Jones."

The count, a little man, with a waxed mustache of extraordinary size, a long nose, and pale, watery eyes, rose, and bowed profoundly.

"I am most happy, Monsieur Jones, to have ze honor of making your acquaintance," he said.

"My lord count, the honor is on my side," returned Alphonso, with an elaborate bow, which he had learned in dancing-school.

"Mr. Jones," said Ingalls, "will you take the chair next to the count? Our distinguished friend is desirous of making some inquiries about fashionable society in America."

"I shall be most happy," replied Alphonso, immensely flattered, "to give the noble count any information in my power."

"I understand from Monsieur Ingalls you do go much in society," said the count.

"A little, your lordship," said Mr. Jones, modestly. "I am intimate in some of our leading families."

"You have some fine watering-places, *n'est ce pas*?"

"Yes, my lord count,—Newport, Saratoga, and Long Branch are all fashionable."

"You have visit zem all?"

"Oh, yes," answered Alphonso, who had once stopped over night at Saratoga, and made a day's excursion to Long Branch. "I meet so many of my fashionable friends there, that it is very pleasant for me."

"*Sans doute*, and which do you prefare?"

"Saratoga, my lord count. It is the most high-toned, in my opinion. My friends, the Vernons, of Madison avenue, always go there."

"I once did know a Marquis de Vernon in my own country."

"A relation of my friends," said Alphonso, confidently. "How long has your lordship been in America?"

"Tree week, zat is all."

"Have you been in New York all the time?"

"No, Monsieur Jones, I did visit Boston and Philadelphia, but New York is one fine city, ze best of all; it reminds me of Paris."

"Paris is a very beautiful city, I have always heard, my lord count."

"Oh, *très magnifique*. Zere is no city like it. Have you visited Paris, Monsieur Alphonse?"

He is getting intimate, thought Mr. Jones, elated, or he would not call me by my first name.

"No, your lordship, I have not had that great pleasure."

"When you come," said the count, affably, "you must come to my chateau in Normandy, and stay one month."

This was beyond Alphonso's most sanguine hopes. To be invited to visit a foreign nobleman at his chateau was an unlooked-for honor.

"You overwhelm me with your kindness, my lord count," said Alphonso, in a flutter of delight. "I hope some day to accept your honorable invitation."

"I think you will have zer good time. My sister, the Countess Marie de Montmorency, will be charmed to see you. She adores Americans."

Alphonso was in the seventh heaven of delight. Instantly he pictured the high-born Countess Marie falling in love with him, marrying him, and thus giving him a place in the aristocratic circles of France. Perhaps, in that case, family influence would procure him a title also. It was the happiest moment of his life.

"Nothing would delight me more than to make the acquaintance of your august family, my lord count," he said, his voice partly tremulous with joy. "When do you propose to return to *la belle France*?"

"What, you do speak my language, Monsieur Alphonse?"

"Only a little, your lordship," said Mr. Jones, modestly.

"*Oui, monsieur, un peu.*"

"*Comment vous portez vous, Monsieur Alphonse?*"

"*Très beaucoup bien*," answered Alphonso, proudly.

"What an accent!" exclaimed the count, raising both hands. "You do speak like one native."

"I think I should soon learn it if I were in *la belle France*," said Alphonso, much pleased.

"Gentlemen," said Mr. Ingalls, "I don't like to interrupt you, but permit me to offer you a glass of wine."

Glasses were handed to the company.

"Mr. Jones, will you propose the count's health?" asked the host. Alphonso rose, and placed one hand on his heart.

"Gentlemen," he commenced, "I feel—ahem! deeply honored, and—and happy on this auspicious occasion. We are assembled, sir, to do honor to an illustrious peer of the realm. The noble Count Ernest de Montmorency honors us with his high-toned presence. We all hope that he may enjoy his visit, and return in safety to his aristocratic relations, his honorable mother, and his sister, the noble Countess Marie de Montmorency. I propose the health of the noble count."

The toast was drunk with enthusiasm.

"Mr. Jones, you are quite an orator," said Mr. Ingalls.

"You have ze great talent for speaking Monsieur Alphonse. You should go to Congress."

"My lord count, you flatter me," said Mr. Jones, deciding that this was, by all odds, the proudest moment of his life.

"Not at all, Mr. Jones," said Mr. Ingalls. "I never heard a neater speech, did you, Hayward?"

"Never," said Hayward.

So poor Alphonso was fooled to the top of his bent, and when the company separated, and he retired to his humble apartment, he was visited by the most ravishing dreams, in which he stood at the altar with the high-born Countess Marie de Montmorency, clad in sumptuous attire, wearing on his breast the cross of the Legion of Honor.

CHAPTER XXIII.

THE LITTLE FLOWER-GIRL.

GILBERT found it very irksome to be without employment; besides, he was anxious to be vindicated as soon as possible from the malicious charge which had been made against him. He felt himself fortunate, however, in one respect; he was subjected to no privations, having his board and lodging paid by his guardian. Had Mr. Briggs suspected him, he was proud enough to have left his boarding-place, and relied upon his own exertions.

From the force of habit, and partly to fill up his time, Gilbert continued to go down-town daily. One day he met Mr. Vivian on Broadway, below the Astor House.

"Good-morning, Gilbert," said the merchant, pleasantly. "Are you out on business?"

"No, sir," answered Gilbert. "I am out of business just at present."

"I thought you were in the office of a stock-broker."

"So I was; but I have lost my place."

"Through no fault of your own, I am sure."

"No, sir. I should not have lost my place if Mr. Sands had been in the city. During his absence the book-keeper, who has a dislike to me because I superseded his cousin, discharged me."

"Come up this evening to my house, Gilbert. Then I shall be at leisure, and you can tell me all the details of the affair."

"Thank you, sir."

"I am sure he won't credit the charge against me," thought Gilbert, and this thought encouraged him not a little.

Gilbert continued his walk. As he was passing Trinity church-yard, he was accosted by a little girl, of perhaps eight years old. "Won't you buy some flowers, sir?—only five cents."

Gilbert shook his head mechanically. Then he glanced at the little girl, and his sympathy was aroused. She was poorly dressed, with a fragile figure, and thin, pale face, which yet only lacked the roundness and rosy hue of health to be uncommonly pretty. She did not repeat her request, but she looked sad and depressed. Gilbert paused and spoke to her.

"Have you sold many flowers to-day, little girl?" he asked.

"No, sir; only three bunches," she replied.

"Where do you get them?"

"I sell them for a woman."

"How much does she give you for selling them?"

"Two cents a bunch."

"Then you have only made six cents to-day. How long have you been standing here?"

"Ever since eight o'clock," said the little girl, wearily.

"Don't you get tired being on your feet so long?"

"I wouldn't care for that if the people would only buy my flowers."

"You are young to be sent out in this way. Haven't you got a father to take care of you?"

"Papa used to take care of me when he was well, and did not let me come out; but now he is sick, and we have no money, and I have to leave him," said the little girl, sadly.

"Poor child!" said Gilbert, compassionately. "You are unfortunate. Where does your father live?"

"On Pearl Street, in a tenement house," said the little flower-girl; "but I am afraid we will be turned out because we cannot pay the rent."

"What is your name?"

"Emma Talbot."

"Then, Emma, if you like, I will go around and see your father with you. Perhaps I can help him, or get some of my friends to help him. Can you come now?"

"When I have sold this bunch of flowers, sir."

"As it is the last you have got, I will take it; so we needn't wait."

"Oh, thank you, sir," said the child, brightening up. "If you won't mind, I will stop and buy a roll at the baker's for papa."

"Certainly, Emma. I have plenty of time. Wait; take my hand while we cross the street, you must be careful, or you may be run over."

"I wait for the policeman generally," said the little girl. "I should be afraid to cross alone."

"You are quite right to be careful."

The little girl took his hand confidingly, and together they crossed the City Hall Park. It was a new sensation to Gilbert to have the charge of a little girl. He had always been thrown among boys, and, never having had a sister, was very ignorant of girls, and the tastes of girls. For the first time, as he held Emma's hand, it occurred to him that he would like to have a little sister, whom he could pet and protect.

As he was crossing the Park, he met his successor, John, sauntering along at a snail's pace. John had been sent out on an errand, but had fallen into his old way of loitering and wasting the time which belonged to his employer. When he caught sight of Gilbert he started in surprise at his young companion.

"Hallo, Greyson!" he said, by way of opening a conversation.

"Good-morning," said Gilbert, coldly.

"Is that your sister?" asked John, looking hard at Emma.

"No," answered Gilbert, shortly.

"Ho, ho!" laughed John. "I understand."

"I am glad you do."

"You've got a place as a girl's nurse. That's good."

"You are very witty," said Gilbert.

"How much wages do you get?" continued John.

"I think I had better not tell you, or you might get up a conspiracy to deprive me of my position."

"What do you mean by that?" asked John, uncomfortably.

"You know well enough what I mean. You know that you got your present place by dishonorable means. But I don't think you'll keep it long."

"You'd better take care what you say," blustered John. "My cousin may have you arrested yet."

"He is quite at liberty to do so," answered Gilbert, unterrified. "I don't think he will find it prudent though."

"Why not?"

"Because it might come out who really put the money in my coat-pocket."

"You did it yourself."

"You are mistaken. I have found out who did put it in."

"Who?"

"I don't think you need any information on that point."

"Look here," said John, angrily, "you'd better not tell any lies to Mr. Sands when he comes back."

"I have no occasion to do so."

"You'd better leave the city, or Mr. Sands may have you arrested."

"I will risk that."

"I guess you can get a place in Philadelphia," said John. "I'll get my cousin to give you a recommendation if you'll promise to go there."

"How can he recommend me after discharging me for theft?"

"He'll think this will be a lesson to you. Shall I ask him?"

"No, thank you. I don't intend to leave the city at present."

"I'm afraid that chap will make trouble for me yet," muttered John to himself, as Gilbert walked away with the little girl; "but he can't prove anything. I guess me and cousin Simon will be more than a match for him."

CHAPTER XXIV.

EMMA'S FATHER.

GILBERT kept on his way with the little girl. After a short walk, she paused in front of a miserable tenement house on Pearl Street.

"This is where we live," she said; "will you go upstairs, sir?"

"If you think I shall not be intruding on your father," said Gilbert, with instinctive delicacy.

"He will be glad to see a kind face," said Emma, simply.

"Then if you will lead the way, I will follow," said our hero.

They clambered up three flights of stairs, and then Emma opened a door and ushered her companion into a small, barely furnished room. On a pallet on the floor was stretched a man of fifty, pale and emaciated, with eyes preternaturally bright; his face was turned towards the wall, and he did not see Gilbert.

"Is that you, Emma?" he asked.

"Yes, papa; how do you feel now?" asked the little girl.

"Much the same, my child; did you sell your flowers?"

"Yes, papa, and I have brought you a fresh roll. I have brought some one with me, too."

Mr. Talbot turned his head, and looked at Gilbert, not without surprise.

"I hope you won't look upon me as an intruder, sir," said Gilbert; "your little girl told me you would not, or I would not have ventured to call."

"I am glad to see you," said the sick man, "though this is but a poor place to receive company in."

"I understand your situation, sir," said Gilbert; "you have been sick and unfortunate."

"You are right; I was unfortunate first, and sick afterwards. Emma, will you give the young gentleman a chair?"

"Oh, don't trouble yourself," said Gilbert, taking a chair for himself.

Mr. Talbot proceeded: "Five years since, I removed to Chicago, with my little girl, in the hope that in that growing and prosperous Western city I might, at least, earn a comfortable living. I was not wholly without means,—I had about a thousand dollars,—but misfortune pursued me. I was once burnt out, lost my situation by the failure of the firm that employed me, and the end of it all was, that a year ago I found myself bankrupt. Then I decided to come to New York, hoping to succeed better here. I managed, while I was well, to earn a precarious living by copying for lawyers (I am a book-keeper by vocation) but, a month since, I was stricken down by a fever, from which I am only just recovering. How we have got along I can hardly tell you. When I became sick I had but a dollar in my pocket-book, yet we have continued to live. My little Emma," he continued, looking proudly at the little girl, "has been a great help to me. She has managed to earn a little, and has attended upon me by night and by day. I don't know what I could have done without her."

"I ought to work for you now, papa," said the child, simply; "all my life you have been working for me."

"She is a perfect little woman, though only ten years old," said the father. "Poor child! her life has been far from bright. I hope the future has some happier days in store for both of us."

"Only get well, sir," said Gilbert, cheerfully, "and the happier days will begin."

"I hope so; but even in health I found it hard to get along."

At this moment there was a knock at the door.

Emma went to the door, and opened it.

A short, stout, coarse-featured woman entered, and looked about her with the air of one who had come to engage in battle.

"Take a seat, Mrs. Flanders," said the sick man.

"Much obliged to you, sir," said the woman, not to be placated by this politeness; "but I can't stop. I come on business. I suppose you know what it is."

"I suppose it is the rent," said Mr. Talbot, uneasily.

"Yes, it is the rent," said Mrs. Flanders. "I hope you are ready to pay it."

"How can you expect it, Mrs. Flanders? You know how long I have been sick and unable to earn anything."

"That is not my fault, Mr. Talbot," said the woman, sharply. "I'm a widow woman, and have to look out for myself. When I let you this room, I told you you must pay me prompt, for I had to pay prompt. Have you forgot that?"

"No, I have not forgotten it, and I am very sorry that circumstances have been so against me. Wait patiently, and I will pay you yet."

"Wait patiently!" repeated the woman, angrily. "Haven't I been waiting patiently for a month? To-morrow I have to pay my rent, and I must be paid what you owe me."

"We have but a few cents in the house," said Mr. Talbot. "How much have you got, Emma?"

"Four cents, papa."

"Give them to Mrs. Flanders; it is all we have."

"Four cents!" exclaimed the landlady, shrilly; "do you mean to insult me?"

"I don't feel much like insulting anybody," said Mr. Talbot, wearily.

"Once more, do you intend to pay me my rent or not?" demanded the virago.

"I can't at present. In time—"

"Stuff and nonsense!—then out you budge to-day. I can't afford to keep you here for nothing."

"O Mrs. Flanders," pleaded Emma, in terror. "It will kill my father to go out, sick as he is. Let us stay here a little longer."

"It won't do," said the woman; "I'm not so soft as that comes to. If you won't pay the rent, you must budge."

Gilbert had listened to this dialogue with mingled pain and indignation. It was his first practical acquaintance with poverty and the world's inhumanity. He could remain silent no longer.

"How much is your bill, madam?" he asked.

"Rent for four weeks, at a dollar a week,—four dollars."

"I will pay it," said Gilbert, glad that the amount was not beyond his resources.

The little girl impulsively seized his hand and carried it to her lips.

"Oh, how kind you are!" she said.

"Are you sure it will not inconvenience you?" asked Mr. Talbot.

"Oh, no, sir."

"Then I will accept the loan with thanks. You are a friend in need."

The landlady took the money with avidity, for she had considered the debt a bad one.

"Thank you, young man," she said; adding, in an apologetic tone, "You may think me hard, but I have to be. I have to live myself."

Gilbert listened coldly, for he was disgusted with the woman's coarse and brutal manners.

"And I hope you'll get well soon, sir," she said, turning to Mr. Talbot; but he did not answer her.

"It is the way of the world," he remarked, after Mrs. Flanders had gone out. "Poverty has few friends."

"When you are well, sir, I will mention you to a friend who may give you some work," said Gilbert. "Meanwhile I will call again in a day or two."

"You will always be welcome," said Mr. Talbot, gratefully. "You have done me a great service."

When Gilbert went out, he realized that his generosity might cause him inconvenience, for he had but a dollar remaining in his pocket-book, and was earning nothing.

CHAPTER XXV.

GILBERT IN A TIGHT PLACE.

GILBERT called upon the Vivians the same evening. He was received with as much cordiality as on his first visit.

"Now," said Mr. Vivian, laying down the evening paper, which he had been reading at Gilbert's entrance, "tell me how you came to lose your place."

Gilbert told his story in the fewest possible words.

"It's a great shame," said Fred, indignantly; "I'd like to put a head on that book-keeper."

"I sympathize with you, Fred," said Laura; "but I think you might have expressed yourself differently."

"Your sister is right, Fred," said Mr. Vivian; "you must not be too ready to employ street phrases."

"That's what I mean, any way," said Fred.

"Do you think your employer will do you justice when he returns?" asked Mr. Vivian.

"Yes, sir. Mr. Sands is an excellent man, and he knows very well that Mr. Moore is prejudiced against me."

"Then you expect to be taken back?"

"Yes, sir."

"If anything should occur to prevent, come at once and let me know."

"Thank you, sir."

Before the evening was over Gilbert managed to introduce the subject of the little flower-girl whom he had befriended. He gave an account of the father's sickness, and the little girl's devotion. Fred and Laura were much interested, and asked many questions, which Gilbert answered as well as he could.

"You think these people really worthy of assistance, Gilbert?" asked Mr. Vivian.

"Yes, sir, I have no doubt of it."

"You know there are many impostors, who live by working on the sympathies of the benevolent?"

"Yes, sir; but in this case I have no hesitation at all. I am sure Mr. Talbot and the little girl deserve help."

"In that case," said the merchant, "I am willing to do something for them."

He drew from his pocket a ten-dollar bill and handed it to Gilbert.

"It may be best," he suggested, "not to give them this money all at once, but a dollar or two at a time, in order to insure its careful use."

"Thank you, sir," said Gilbert, joyfully; "this money will be like a fortune to them. I will see that your wishes are carried out."

"Papa," said Fred, "may I give Gilbert my five-dollar gold piece for the little girl and her father?"

"Not at present, Fred; though I am glad you feel like offering it. When this money is expended, Gilbert will let us know, and then we will see what else is to be done."

"You are a dear, good boy, to offer the money," said Laura, giving her brother an unexpected kiss; "you have got a good heart, though you don't always keep your face and hands clean."

"A fellow can't be always washing his face and hands," said Fred. "You needn't kiss me if you are afraid of the dirt."

Laura laughed. "I will risk it this time," she said.

"Won't you play me a game of checkers, Gilbert?" asked Fred.

"What am I to do while you two are playing?" asked Laura.

"Oh, you can be umpire," said Fred.

"I should be sure to decide against you," said Laura.

"That's because you like Gilbert," said Fred, who was just at the age when a boy is apt to make disconcerting speeches.

Laura blushed a little, and so did Gilbert.

"I think we both like him," said Laura.

"I do," said Fred.

"Thank you both," said Gilbert. "I suppose there isn't such a thing as three playing a game of checkers. That would bring us all in."

"No," said Laura; "but we can play the Mansion of Happiness, if Fred is willing."

"I don't mind," said Fred. "That's good fun, too."

So the game referred to was brought out, and an hour was consumed in this way. Fred, to his great delight, was the victor each time, and was disposed to exult over his vanquished opponents.

"Never mind, Fred; it will be our turn next time," said Laura.

At half-past nine Gilbert set out for home. He felt that he had passed a pleasant evening, and was cheered by the thought that his discharge had not alienated these true friends from him.

Two days later he went into the office of Mr. Briggs. He was accustomed to make a weekly call, when Mr. Briggs would give him money to pay his week's board.

"Is Mr. Briggs in?" he asked, after looking about him in vain for that gentleman.

"Mr. Briggs will not be in for a long time," said the clerk addressed. "He has gone to Europe."

"Gone to Europe!" exclaimed Gilbert, in genuine astonishment.

"Business of importance called him very suddenly," said the clerk.

"How long is he to be gone?"

"It is uncertain. From two to three months, I should say."

"Did he leave any letter or message for me,—Gilbert Greyson?"

The clerk shook his head.

"Nothing at all," he answered.

Gilbert left the office in great perplexity. How was he to pay the week's board now due, he asked himself, with less than a dollar in hand, and no income?

CHAPTER XXVI.

THE COUNT'S SECRET.

ON the morning after Alphonso Jones had enjoyed his memorable interview with the Count Ernest de Montmorency, he bore himself in a loftier and more consciously superior manner than usual. He felt that he was entitled to a larger measure of consideration, on account of his intimacy with one of the nobility.

"The count must have seen something in me, or he would not have invited me to visit him at his chateau," reflected Alphonso.

It was natural that Mr. Jones should wish his friends to be aware of his social distinction.

"Good-morning, Mr. Kidder," he said, in a patronizing manner, to his fellow-clerk. "How did you enjoy the theatre last evening?"

"Very well. The play was a good one, and well performed."

"I also passed the evening in a very agreeable manner," remarked Alphonso, complacently.

"Where were you?"

"In Mr. Ingalls' room."

"Oh, yes, I forgot. What company did he have in? Didn't you say something of a French count being expected?"

"The Count Ernest de Montmorency was present," said Alphonso, dwelling with unction on the high-sounding syllables.

"How did you like him?" asked Kidder, who had received a brief note from Mr. Ingalls, letting him into the secret.

"I never met a more high-toned gentleman," said Mr. Jones, enthusiastically. "His manners were most courtly, and I may add that he was very affable to me."

"Ingalls ought to have invited me," said Mr. Kidder, affecting to feel slighted.

"He will doubtless remember you another time," said Alphonso; "probably the count does not like a large company."

"I suppose he is just like other men," said Kidder, by way of drawing out his fellow-clerk. "If you hadn't known him to be a count, you wouldn't have seen anything particular in him."

"I beg to differ with you," said Alphonso, with an air of superior information. "*Some* persons might have thought so; but I claim to be a judge of men, and I at once saw that he was a high-toned aristocrat."

"What did you judge from, now?" asked Kidder, amused.

"I cannot explain what,—it was that the French call *je ne sais quoi*," answered Mr. Jones, who had been studying up some French phrases that very morning.

"*Genesee squaw!*" echoed Kidder, purposely misunderstanding him. "What on earth has a French count to do with a Genesee squaw?"

"I pity your ignorance, Mr. Kidder," said Alphonso, mildly. "The words I used were French, and mean, 'I don't know what.'"

"You don't know what they mean? Then why do you use them?"

"You misunderstand me again. *Je ne sais quoi* means I—do—not—know—what. Do you see it now?"

"Oh, that's it. I didn't know you were such a French scholar, Mr. Jones."

"I am a poor French scholar," said Alphonso, modestly; "but I shall try to make myself familiar with the language before I go to France."

"Are you going to France? How long has that been in your mind?"

"To tell the truth, Mr. Kidder, I never thought seriously of it till last evening. But since the Count de Montmorency has been kind enough to invite me to visit him at his chateau, and become acquainted with his noble family, I feel that it is quite worth my while to prepare myself to converse with them."

"You don't say so! What a lucky fellow you are! Did the count really invite you?"

"He invited me in the most affable and friendly—I may say urgent manner," said Alphonso, complacently.

"Couldn't you get me an invitation, too?" asked Kidder, in pretended anxiety. "I've been long wanting to go abroad, and I think my father would consent, if I received such an invitation as that."

"I should like to oblige you, Mr. Kidder, but really I couldn't venture on such a liberty," said Alphonso, decidedly; for he feared that his fellow-clerk, who was better-looking than himself, might interfere with his matrimonial designs upon the count's high-born sister.

"Perhaps the count will invite me himself. I'll get Ingalls to introduce me."

"Possibly," said Alphonso, coldly; "but I wouldn't obtrude myself upon his lordship."

"I don't see why I shouldn't be introduced as well as you."

Alphonso, who privately considered himself more high-toned than Kidder, felt that there was good reason, but did not think it policy to pursue the subject.

Probably Mr. Jones referred to the Count Ernest de Montmorency at least thirty times that day, and succeeded in arousing the curiosity and envy of such of his acquaintances as were not in the secret. He indulged in many a gorgeous day-dream, in which he figured as the brother-in-law of the count, with a beautiful chateau of his own, and this continued for several days. But his dreams were destined to a rude awakening.

One evening, in passing through Bleeker Street, Mr. Jones strolled into a barber shop, which he had never before entered. He glanced carelessly about him, when he made a sudden start, and gasped for breath. There, behind a barber's chair, in the act of shaving a red-headed man, was the elegant Count Ernest de Montmorency!

The count looked up and met Alphonso's astonished gaze.

"Good-evening, M. Alphonse," he said, with a nod and a smile.

"Good-evening," ejaculated Alphonso, with difficulty.

How could he say "my lord count" to a barber?

"Are you the—the—gentleman I met at the room of my friend, Mr. Ingalls?" asked Mr. Jones.

"The same. I will explain hereafter," said the count, mysteriously.

Alphonso succeeded the red-headed man in the chair presided over by the count.

"I am incognito," said the latter, in a low voice. "I have been reduced to poverty by the rascality of a relative. They don't know me here in the shop."

"You don't say so!" ejaculated Mr. Jones, much impressed.

"They think I am a common man. It would not do to tell them."

"Does Mr. Ingalls know?" asked Alphonso.

"Yes, he knows how I am reduced; but he does not respect me the less. May I rely upon your secrecy, also?"

"Certainly, my lord—I mean, sir," said Mr. Jones, beginning to think it was all right again. "Do you think you will ever recover your estates?"

"Don't speak so loud! Yes, I am almost sure of it. In that case, I shall expect you to visit me at my chateau."

"Thank you. I shall be most happy."

"How strange it seems to be shaved by a count!" thought Alphonso. "But I really wish he wasn't a barber. Couldn't he get something else to do?"

"How is your friend, the Count de Montmorency, Mr. Jones?" asked Mr. Kidder, the next morning.

"I believe he is well," said Alphonso, shortly.

CHAPTER XXVII.

HARD UP.

A STREET boy, accustomed to live from hand to mouth, would not have been disconcerted on finding himself in Gilbert's circumstances. But this was our hero's first experience of debt which he was unable to pay, and it troubled him. He felt embarrassed at the dinner-table, knowing that he was eating a meal for which he had not the means of paying; and this thought not only interfered with his appetite, but made him unusually silent and reserved. His room-mate noticed this, and spoke of it when they had gone up to their room together.

"What made you so quiet, Gilbert?" he asked. "You scarcely uttered a word at the dinner-table."

"The fact is, Mr. Ingalls, I am in trouble," answered Gilbert.

"About your loss of place? You told me about that, and that you expected to get it back when your employer returned."

"So I do; but there is another trouble."

"Troubles never come singly, they say."

"It seems to be true in my case. I am owing for a week's board, and don't know where I shall get the money to pay it."

"I thought your guardian paid your board," said Ingalls, who was acquainted with the particulars of Gilbert's history.

"So he did; but he has sailed for Europe suddenly, without making any provision for the payment of my money."

"How long is he to be gone?"

"Two or three months, they told me at the office."

"That is rather inconvenient. If you were only a few years older, there would be a remedy."

"What remedy?"

"You could marry Miss Brintnall. Mrs. White told me the other day that Miss Brintnall has saved up two or three thousand dollars from her earnings."

"That will be convenient for you when she becomes Mrs. Ingalls," said Gilbert, with a smile.

"Do you think I would sacrifice myself for that paltry sum?" demanded Ingalls, with much indignation. "Ten thousand dollars is the lowest sum for which I will sacrifice my liberty. I'll tell you who is most likely to become Miss Brintnall's husband, that is, if she consents."

"Who?"

"Alphonso Jones."

"What makes you think so?"

"Alphonso lacks money to back up his gentility. He only gets twelve dollars a week, Kidder tells me, though he claims to have a thousand dollars a year. Miss Brintnall's fortune will be a great inducement to him."

"You forget that he has hopes of an alliance with the sister of the Count de Montmorency."

"I think he had better take Miss Brintnall," said Mr. Ingalls, dryly. "Now, to come back to your affairs. Are you quite out of money?"

"Almost. I gave four dollars to a poor family a day or two since, not expecting that I was to be left this way. I have about fifty cents in my pocket-book, and I owe a week's board."

His room-mate reflected a moment.

"I wish I were richer, for your sake, Gilbert," he said. "As it is, I can lend you money enough to pay this week's board bill. Before another week comes round, something may turn up."

"Thank you," said Gilbert, gratefully; "but I don't like to rob you."

"You won't rob me, for I intend to let you repay it when you can. If I could keep it up till your guardian returns I would do so; but this I can't do. I will tell you what I would do in your case."

"I wish you would advise me, for I don't know what to do. I never was in such a situation before."

"It was understood that your guardian would pay your board for the present, was it not?"

"Yes. He offered to do it. I never would have asked him."

"You say he left no directions at the office in regard to it?"

"So the chief clerk told me."

"It is clear, then, that it escaped his mind in the hurry of an unexpected departure. Probably he will set the matter right in his first letter. Wait a minute, though. His wife and son probably accompanied him to the steamer to see him off."

"I suppose so."

"Very likely he spoke to them about it. I advise you to call on them and inquire."

Gilbert looked reluctant.

"It may be as you say," said he; "but I don't like to speak to Mrs. Briggs on the subject. She dislikes me, and so I think does Randolph, though not so much as his mother."

"So you have told me; still I advise you to call, the sooner the better, in my opinion."

"Suppose I get no satisfaction?"

"In that case you will know what to look forward to. If you are thrown upon your own resources, you can lay your plans accordingly."

"I should like to know the worst, at any rate," said Gilbert, thoughtfully.

"Then take my advice, and call this evening on Mrs. Briggs."

"I will," said Gilbert; "but I would rather have a tooth out."

CHAPTER XXVIII.

AN UNSATISFACTORY CALL.

MR. INGALLS was right in his conjecture. On board the steamer Mr. Briggs had thought of his young ward, and was rather annoyed that he had not left directions at the office that he should be paid his regular weekly stipend.

"There is one thing which I have forgotten," he said to his wife.

"What is it?" she inquired.

"Gilbert has been in the habit of coming to me every week for his board. I ought to have left directions at the office with Seymour to pay him in my place."

He forgot that Mrs. Briggs was not aware of this arrangement. She was not slow in expressing her dissatisfaction.

"You don't mean to say that that boy lived on you!" she exclaimed.

"I pay his board, if that is what you mean by living on me."

"That is what it amounts to. Why permit this?"

"Surely, you don't expect that Gilbert will pay all his expenses out of five dollars a week," said her husband.

"Why can't he get along as well as other boys?"

"Other boys have no friends able to help them. Gilbert's father was my friend, and I mean to stand by him."

"How much do you allow him for board?"

"Six dollars a week."

"Can't he get boarded cheaper?"

"It seems to me that six dollars is very cheap. You remember that I spent a hundred dollars a week for you and Randolph and myself at Saratoga one season. That is about thirty-three dollars apiece."

"There is no resemblance in the two cases," said Mrs. Briggs, coldly. "Gilbert Greyson is only a working-boy."

"And I am a working-man."

"Don't talk foolishly, Mr. Briggs," said his wife, sharply.

"I have not much time to talk foolishly or otherwise. Will you attend to this matter of Gilbert's board?"

"I will attend to it," said Mrs. Briggs.

"Then there will be no need of my writing to the office."

"No, there will be no occasion to trouble yourself further in the matter."

On this assurance Mr. Briggs dismissed Gilbert from his mind, and shortly afterwards bade good-by to his wife and son.

"I sometimes think your father is actually soft," said Mrs. Briggs to Randolph, on the way over the ferry. "What claim has that Greyson boy upon him, that he should squander six dollars a week upon him? And that isn't all, I presume. I have no doubt the boy manages to coax extra money out of him almost every week."

"He won't get it out of you, mother," said Randolph.

"I should say not," said Mrs. Briggs, very emphatically. "I should feel that I was robbing you. If your father impoverishes himself by such ill-timed liberality, you will be the sufferer."

"I didn't think of that," said Randolph, soberly.

"I don't, of course, wish to be mean or parsimonious," continued Mrs. Briggs, "but I hold that a man's first duty is to his own family."

"Of course it is," said Randolph, who felt confident of it now that he saw the bearing upon his own interests.

"Will you give Gilbert the six dollars a week?" he inquired.

"Not unless he asks for it," said Mrs. Briggs. "If he doesn't need it there will be no occasion to offer it."

"If he don't ask for it, will you give it to me?" asked Randolph.

"You have an allowance of five dollars a week now. It seems to me that ought to be sufficient."

"I can't save anything from it. If you give me the six dollars beside, I'll put some in the savings bank."

"I will wait and see whether the boy calls for it."

"I hope he won't."

"He probably will. He'll take all he can get. That is his nature."

Mrs. Briggs quite misread Gilbert, as my readers will probably judge; but she was too prejudiced to judge him fairly.

Randolph was not as mean as his mother. He had a little of his father's nature, though he was more like his mother. The thought that it would impair his future inheritance did not much affect him, but the prospect of having his allowance so largely increased took away all consideration for Gilbert. He cared very little whether our hero was able to pay his board or not, if only the money might be paid to him. He was very selfish certainly; but he loved money for what it would buy, and not for its own sake, as was the case with his mother. Of course he hoped that Gilbert would not present himself at the house, or make inquiry for the money; but in this he was destined to be disappointed.

Sitting at the window on the evening Gilbert had resolved to call, he saw, not without disappointment, our hero mount the steps and ring the bell.

"He's come, mother," said he, in a tone of regret.

"Who has come?"

"Gilbert Greyson. I suppose he has come for his six dollars."

"I suppose he has," said Mrs. Briggs, with a curl of the lip. "I knew he wouldn't keep away long. Now, Randolph, one thing I ask,—don't say a word about the matter. I want to make him introduce the subject himself. I don't wish to spare him any embarrassment."

"All right, mother."

Directly the door opened, and Gilbert entered.

"Good-evening, Mrs. Briggs," he said, approaching and taking the lady's hand. She just touched his hand coldly, and withdrew hers.

"Good-evening," she said, briefly.

"Good-evening, Randolph," said Gilbert, turning to the younger member of the party.

"Good-evening," said Randolph, less frigidly. "Have you got a place yet?"

"Not yet. My employer has not returned from Washington."

"Probably it will make very little difference to you how long he stays," said Mrs. Briggs, disagreeably.

"I hope it will make considerable," returned Gilbert. "I was surprised to hear that Mr. Briggs had gone to Europe."

"He went very suddenly," said Randolph. "It has put off my birthday party."

"I should like to have seen him before he went," said Gilbert.

"He had no time to notify all his acquaintances that he was going," said Mrs. Briggs.

"How long will he be gone?"

"It is quite uncertain," said the lady, shortly. "It will depend on his business, of course."

"I wish this visit were well over," thought Gilbert, but he felt that he must introduce the matter which led to his call.

"Did Mr. Briggs leave any message for me?" he inquired.

"Any message for you?" repeated Mrs. Briggs, arching her eyebrows. "Why should you expect that he would leave any message for you?"

"Perhaps you are not aware," said Gilbert, uncomfortably, "that Mr. Briggs, while I am at work on small wages, has been in the habit of paying my board."

"Indeed!" said Mrs. Briggs, in apparent surprise. "Why should he do that?"

"Out of friendship for my father, he told me," said Gilbert.

"I should hardly have supposed that you would request such a thing of one not related to you."

"I didn't request it," said Gilbert, coloring. "Mr. Briggs was kind enough to offer to do it. I accepted, on condition that I might hereafter repay him what money he should advance."

"It is not very likely the money will ever be repaid," said Mrs. Briggs, coldly.

"It will be repaid if I live," said Gilbert, warmly.

"I have heard such promises before," said the lady, contemptuously. "They are generally made to be broken."

"Not in my case," said Gilbert, flushing.

"I will not discuss the matter," said Mrs. Briggs, coldly. "May I ask why you have introduced this subject?"

"Mr. Briggs gave me no notice that he intended to withdraw his assistance, and I accordingly went to the office yesterday, only to learn that he had gone to Europe, and left no message there. I thought he might possibly have spoken to you on the subject, and therefore I called. My board-bill, amounting to six dollars, is due to-night, and unfortunately I have no funds to meet it."

"It must be rather humiliating for you to accept charity," said Mrs. Briggs. "I don't think my son would be willing to do it."

"I should say not," said Randolph.

"Say nothing more, Mrs. Briggs," said Gilbert, rising. "If you regard it in that light, I wish no assistance."

"I don't wish you to suffer," continued Mrs. Briggs, coldly. "I will give you money for your board-bill, if you will tell me how much it amounts to."

"Thank you, I won't trouble you," said Gilbert. "I shall get along somehow. Good-evening."

"You are impetuous. You will bear in mind that I have not refused you the money."

"I will bear it in mind. Good-evening, madam."

"You did it well, mother," said Randolph, admiringly, as our hero left the house. "Will you give me the six dollars, now he has refused it?"

"I will give it to you this week, Randolph; but mind, I make no promises for the future."

"I guess it's all right," thought Randolph, pocketing the bills complacently. "I'll take care she keeps it up."

CHAPTER XXIX.

GILBERT'S PLANS.

GILBERT left the house of Mrs. Briggs, not cast down, but with a full understanding of his situation. Until now he had had his guardian's assistance, and, with the income from his position as office-boy, had felt no anxiety. Now, both had failed him, for the time at least, and he must shift for himself. Disaster develops the manhood in a boy as well as a man. So Gilbert did not indulge in any gloomy anticipations of starvation or pauperism. He never for a moment regretted his refusal to take money from Mrs. Briggs, offered as it had been in such a manner as to insult his self-respect.

"I'd rather live on one meal a day," he said to himself stoutly, "than humble myself to that woman."

When he re-entered his room he found his room-mate reading.

"Well, Gilbert," he said, "did you have a pleasant call?"

"So pleasant that I shall not call again in a hurry," answered Gilbert.

"Then Mrs. Briggs won't give you any assistance?"

"Yes; but I have rejected it."

Mr. Ingalls looked surprised.

"Did you not act unwisely?" he asked.

"Let me tell you just what passed between us, and you shall judge."

The young man listened attentively. When Gilbert had finished his story, he said, emphatically, "You did just right. I should have done the same thing in your circumstances."

"I am glad you approve of my action. I couldn't stoop to take money offered as charity."

"Then you have got to strike out for yourself, it seems?"

"Yes, and I must settle to-night what I shall do."

"Have you made up your mind to anything?"

"I was thinking about that as I walked home. To begin with, I will borrow money of you to pay Mrs. White, if you are still willing to lend it."

"I will lend it to you with pleasure."

"I think I had better leave this house, obtain a cheaper room, and board at a restaurant."

"I don't think you can save much that way. Mrs. White is very reasonable in her charges."

"I know that, but the probability is that I can't pay her. I must be strictly economical. I am not sure but the best thing I can do is to go to the Newsboys' Lodge."

Mr. Ingalls shook his head.

"It would never do," he said. "It would not suit a boy brought up as you have been."

"I don't suppose it would; but I don't expect to suit myself. That is not the question with me. I must do as I can."

"Then stay here. If you can't pay your whole board at the week's end I will make up the balance. I should have to pay more, at any rate, if I occupied the room alone."

Gilbert reflected a moment.

"You are very kind, Mr. Ingalls," he said, "and I will accept your offer, on one condition."

"What is that?"

"That you lend me the money, and I will repay it as soon as I am able."

"I agree to that."

"Then I will stay, for a week or two at least. Now I want to ask your advice. I must find something to do at once."

"I wish there was a vacancy in our establishment."

"I only want temporary employment. I expect Mr. Sands will take me back on his return."

"I didn't think of that. Have you thought of anything?"

"I am going to try my luck as a newsboy."

"As a newsboy! What will your friends, the Vivians, say?"

"I don't know, and I can't afford to care. I must get a living somehow for the next few days, and I would rather sell papers than black boots. In the afternoon I shall try to get a little baggage-smashing to do."

"I admire your pluck, Gilbert," said his room-mate. "Not many boys, brought up as you have been, would be willing to sell papers in the streets."

"I don't pretend to like it," said Gilbert; "but I would rather do it than sponge on others, or take money flung at me as alms. If you object to rooming with a common newsboy," he added, smiling, "I suppose I must look for another boarding-place."

"Wait till I give you notice to quit," said Ingalls. "In the mean time I will do all I can to encourage you. I will buy a morning paper of you to-morrow morning. Where shall you stand?"

"Near the 'Times' building, I think. Don't forget your promise now. If I have one customer engaged I shall sleep more soundly."

"You can rely upon me. Have you got money enough to start yourself in business? If not, command my purse."

"I will borrow fifty cents, to make sure that I have enough. Now, as I must be up betimes and take an early breakfast, I think I will turn in."

"Good-night, then. I will stay up and read awhile longer."

"He's a plucky boy," thought the young man. "He deserves to succeed, and I believe he will."

CHAPTER XXX.

GILBERT BECOMES A NEWSBOY.

AT an early hour the next morning Gilbert took his stand near the office of the daily "Times." He attracted immediate attention from the members of the new profession in which he had enrolled himself without permission.

"What are you doin' here?" asked Jim Noonan, a tall newsboy, with red hair and freckled face.

"I am selling papers," answered Gilbert, quietly.

"What business have you here anyhow? That's my place."

"I shall not interfere with you."

"You'd better not," said Jim, pugnaciously, under the impression that Gilbert was apologising. "Just you leave here!"

Gilbert eyed him quietly.

"I shall not interfere with you," he repeated; "nor will I allow you to interfere with me," he added, firmly.

Jim looked at him attentively, and his opinion of him was somewhat altered.

"What does a boy with good clothes want selling papers?" he asked.

"He wants to make a living," said Gilbert. "Paper, sir?"

The man addressed purchased a four-cent paper. Gilbert made change in a business-like manner, and directly afterwards sold another, while Jim Noonan looked on enviously.

"I've a good mind to bust your head," he said, angrily.

"Better go to work and look for customers," suggested Gilbert, coolly.

Jim eyed him with angry discontent. He would like to have pitched into him, but Gilbert was compactly made, and, though smaller than his fellow-newsboy, looked difficult to handle. Jim had hoped to frighten him; but his success was not encouraging.

Gilbert, on the whole, succeeded beyond his anticipations. Probably his appearance was in his favor, and attracted customers. But this was not all. He was quick and alert in manner, and kept a good look-out for trade.

"How many papers have you sold?" asked Jim, after a while.

"Fifty," answered Gilbert.

"Fifty!" ejaculated Jim; "why, I aint sold but twenty."

"You haven't attended to business as closely as I have."

"Ef it hadn't been for you I'd have sold a good many more."

"That isn't the reason. You would have sold as many as I if you had tried as hard."

"It's mean, a boy like you comin' down, and takin' away a poor boy's business."

"I shan't sell papers any longer than I have to. I hope next week to go into something else."

Just then a gentleman inquired for a paper which Gilbert was out of.

"I think he's got it," said Gilbert, pointing to Jim, thereby obtaining a customer for the latter.

"We may as well help each other," said Gilbert. "There's no use in quarrelling."

"Do you mean that?" asked Jim, doubtfully.

"Yes, I do."

"You aint as mean as I thought you was," said Jim, his dislike beginning to evaporate.

"I hope you'll stick to that opinion," said Gilbert, good-humoredly. "When I go out of this business I'll recommend my friends to patronize you."

Thus far Gilbert had seen no one whom he knew. That trial was yet to come. I call it a trial, because Gilbert was quite aware that in becoming a newsboy he had made a descent in the social scale. He had taken the step as a matter of necessity, and not because he liked it. He knew very well how it would be regarded by his acquaintances, and he rather dreaded the expressions of surprise which it would elicit.

The first acquaintance to greet him was Alphonso Jones.

"Good gracious, Greyson!" he exclaimed, "what are you doing here?"

"Selling papers," answered Gilbert, flushing a little.

"I thought you was in a broker's office."

"So I was, and hope to be again; but just now I'm out of a place, so I've gone into business on my own account."

"But, good gracious, how can you sell papers?"

"It's the only thing that offered, and I must earn my living."

"Suppose the Count Ernest de Montmorency should see you,—what would he say?"

"I hope he would buy a paper of me," returned Gilbert, smiling.

"And your friends, the Vivians,—they would be awfully shocked."

"I can't help it. I must earn a living. Won't you have a paper, Mr. Jones? I've got all the morning papers—'Times,' 'Tribune,' 'Herald,' 'Sun.'"

"I'm afraid I haven't got any change," said Alphonso, whose large expenditure for clothing compelled him to economize on minor matters. "But, really, now, you aint going to keep the thing up, are you?"

"Till I get something better," said Gilbert, firmly. "I hope that will be soon. I don't like it myself."

"It's so—so ungentlemanly a business."

"I don't agree with you, Mr. Jones; I think it perfectly respectable."

"Oh, yes, of course; but it is not high-toned, you'll admit that."

"Perhaps not," said Gilbert, with a smile. "I don't pretend to be a judge of what is high-toned. I hope you won't cut my acquaintance, Mr. Jones, because I am a newsboy."

"Oh, no, of course not; but I am afraid your friends, the Vivians, will."

"I hope not," said Gilbert.

Alphonso Jones departed, and next in order came John,—Gilbert's successor at the broker's.

"Oh, my eye!" he exclaimed, in genuine astonishment; "you don't mean to say you've turned newsboy?"

"Yes, I have. Will you buy a paper?"

"Haven't got a cent. How's business?" asked John, with a grin.

"Pretty good."

"Hope you've got a permanent situation."

"I think not. I don't expect to sell papers more than a week."

"What are you going to do then?"

"Going back into the office."

"What office?"

"Mr. Sands' office."

"Do you think he'd take back a—"

"Stop there!" said Gilbert, sternly. "You know very well the charge against me is false. Fortunately I am in a position to prove it."

"You are?" asked John, in alarm.

"Yes."

"How can you prove it?"

"I will let you know when the time comes."

John was not disposed to continue the conversation. He walked back to the office, and told Simon Moore that Gilbert was selling papers in the square.

"I am glad his pride is brought low," said Moore, with satisfaction.

"But it isn't," said John. "He is as proud as ever. He says he is coming back here."

"Let him talk," said the book-keeper, contemptuously. "That is all it will amount to."

But John did not feel quite certain of this.

CHAPTER XXXI.

GILBERT'S SECOND DAY.

"HOW much did you make in your new business, Gilbert?" inquired his room-mate, Ingalls, with interest, at the close of his first day's experience.

"Seventy-five cents," answered Gilbert.

"That is quite fair."

"I suppose it is all I could reasonably expect, but it won't pay my expenses. At that rate my weekly income will be but four dollars and a half, while, as you know, my board amounts to six dollars."

"I will pay the extra dollar and a half."

"You are a true friend, Mr. Ingalls," said Gilbert, gratefully, "but that doesn't dispose of all my difficulties. I shall have no money for washing, or to purchase clothing."

"But you expect to get your place back in a week."

"Even if I do, my income will be only five dollars. I never supposed it was so difficult to make a living before."

"Wait and hope, Gilbert," said his room-mate, cheerfully. "That is what I had to do when I first came to the city. It was weeks before I got anything to do at all. I got almost discouraged. Finally, through the influence of a friend, I got a foothold, and have been able to live comfortably ever since."

"I won't get discouraged just yet, at any rate," said Gilbert. "I will wait and see how things come out. If I am forced to remain in the paper business, I must find some way of increasing my income. I might combine a little baggage-smashing with it."

"That's one thing I like about you, Gilbert," said the young man. "You have no false shame, but undertake whatever work you find to do."

"I am not wholly without pride, Mr. Ingalls; but I can't afford to indulge it. I shall get out of this street business as soon as I can."

"You are justified in that, certainly. It shows a proper ambition."

The next day Gilbert sought his chosen place, and again proceeded to sell his stock of daily papers, with about the same measure of success.

At about half-past ten he caught sight of a familiar face. His own face blushed uncomfortably, for Randolph Briggs was about the last person he wished to see, under the circumstances.

Randolph, who was rather near-sighted, did not recognize him till he was close upon him. Gilbert had a momentary impulse to desert his post, and thus escape the notice of his unwelcome acquaintance; but this impulse was succeeded by the more manly resolve to stand his ground.

"I have nothing to be ashamed of," he said to himself. "It is Randolph, or rather his mother, who should be ashamed."

He was in the act of selling a "Herald" when Randolph came up.

"Gilbert Greyson!" exclaimed Randolph, in amazement.

"Good-morning, Randolph," said Gilbert, quietly.

"What are you doing?"

"Selling papers, as you see."

"You don't mean to say you have become a common newsboy?"

"I don't know whether I am a common or uncommon newsboy, but a newsboy I certainly am, just at present."

"What induced you to take up such a business?"

"The necessity of making a living."

"Why didn't you take the money my mother offered you?"

"Because she offered it as charity. I don't accept charity."

"It seems to me you are poor and proud."

"I certainly am poor, and my pride I hope is a proper one."

"I should be too proud to sell papers in the streets," said Randolph, emphatically.

"Perhaps you wouldn't in my case."

"I never expect to be in your case."

"I hope you won't."

"You know, of course, you will have to give up your fashionable acquaintances."

"Does that mean you and your mother?" inquired Gilbert, smiling.

"Yes partly," answered Randolph, seriously. "Then, there are the Vivians. You wouldn't presume to call upon them now?"

"Why not?"

"Do you suppose they admit newsboys in the list of their visitors?"

"I don't know; but I shall soon find out."

"How?"

"I mean to call there very soon."

"I wouldn't. You wouldn't be welcome."

"How do you know that?"

"It stands to reason," argued Randolph. "They stand very high in the social scale, and a newsboy is very low."

"I don't think the Vivians and you quite agree in some matters. If I find I am not welcome, you may be sure I won't repeat the call."

"You will see I am right."

"I suppose, from what you say, that I shall not be welcome at your house?" said Gilbert, rather amused.

"Why, you might call when no one is there. Of course, we couldn't introduce you to our friends."

"I think the safest way will be not to call at all."

"That's so," said Randolph, and he walked on.

"I suppose that is the way of the world," thought Gilbert. "Well, I expected it, and so far as Randolph and his mother are concerned I shall not have much to regret."

At half-past twelve he stood with his last paper in his hand. They had gone off more slowly than the day before, and he doubted whether he could dispose of the last one.

"Good-morning, Gilbert," said a cordial voice. "Are you reading the paper?"

"No, Mr. Vivian," answered our hero; "I am trying to sell it."

"What! Have you turned newsboy?"

"Yes, sir. I could think of nothing else to do, and I must do something."

"Was this necessary?" asked the merchant, in a tone of sympathy.

"Yes, sir; I have nothing to depend upon, except what I make in this way."

"You can't make a living, can you?"

"I am afraid not by this alone," said Gilbert.

"Have you had lunch?"

"No, sir."

"Then come with me to the Astor House restaurant. There we will talk over your affairs, and perhaps I can suggest something that will be more to your advantage than your present employment."

"Thank you, sir; I shall feel very grateful for your advice."

They went to the Astor House, which was very near, and seated themselves at a table. Mr. Vivian ordered a substantial lunch, considerably better than Gilbert could have afforded on his own account. In fact, he had decided to content himself with an apple, and make that do till the six-o'clock dinner at his boarding-house.

CHAPTER XXXII.

A NOVEL PROPOSITION.

A LIBERAL lunch was ordered, and placed before them.

"My time is limited," said Mr. Vivian, "and we will economize it by discussing lunch and your affairs at the same time. How much do you pay for board?"

"Six dollars a week," answered Gilbert.

"That is very little," said the merchant.

"I room with another person, and thus secure more favorable terms."

"Are your meals satisfactory?"

"The food is plain, but good. I have nothing to complain of. I should like nothing better than to feel sure that I could continue to pay my expenses at this rate."

"That is well," said Mr. Vivian, approvingly. "I like your spirit. You are not disposed to find unnecessary fault. Then you cannot make six dollars a week by selling papers?"

"No, sir; at least, I have not done so thus far. Yesterday I made seventy cents, and to-day about the same sum."

"That will never do. It leaves you nothing for washing or clothes."

"No, sir. However, I am pretty well provided with clothes. I don't expect to require anything in that line for six months."

"Probably you couldn't put off washing for so long," suggested Mr. Vivian, with a smile.

"Hardly," answered Gilbert.

"Before you came to the city," said Mr. Vivian, apparently changing the subject, "you were studying for college, were you not?"

"Yes, sir."

"How far had you proceeded?"

"By next summer I could easily have been ready to enter Yale College; if necessary, earlier."

"Then you must be a good classical scholar already."

"A fair one," said Gilbert, modestly.

"Did you ever think of teaching?"

Gilbert looked surprised.

"I don't know who would employ a boy like me," he said.

"You would be competent to instruct a beginner in Latin and the common English studies, I suppose?"

"I ought to be, sir."

"Then I will tell you an idea I have had in mind for a week or more. My boy Fred is attending a classical school, but his progress is not satisfactory to me. I don't think him lacking in capacity, but he does not apply himself as he ought. It has occurred to me that assistance in the evening would materially aid him, and promote his standing in school. Except in Latin I could myself assist him, but after the business and perplexities of the day I am in no mood to turn teacher. Now, you are competent, and Fred has taken a fancy to you. Are you willing to give him five evenings a week?"

"Nothing would suit me better, sir," said Gilbert, quickly. "I like Fred, and would do my best to be of service to him."

Mr. Vivian looked pleased.

"Then," he said, "I see no reason why we should not try the experiment. The only thing remaining to be discussed is the compensation."

"I leave that to you, sir."

"I may take advantage of your confidence," said the merchant.

"I don't feel alarmed," said Gilbert, smiling.

"Suppose, then, we say ten dollars a week for five evenings."

"Ten dollars!" exclaimed Gilbert, in amazement.

"If that is not adequate—"

"Why, Mr. Vivian, my services would never be worth ten dollars a week. Remember, sir, I am only a boy, and inexperienced as a teacher."

"I believe you will do Fred more good than an older and more experienced teacher. He takes to you, and will work cheerfully with you, while I don't think he would with the other."

"But ten dollars a week is a large sum for you to pay, Mr. Vivian."

"I believe in paying a good price, and requiring good, faithful work, such as I think you will render."

"I will try to render it, at any rate, sir."

"Then it is a bargain, is it?"

"Yes, sir, if you say so. I need not say that it will be a very great help to me."

"I know that, Gilbert; and I am glad to be able to serve you, at the same time that I serve myself. When I was a boy I was in limited circumstances. The memory of my own past makes me considerate of others. Now, when will you begin?"

"This evening, if you like."

"I should like it. We will expect you then. Here is a week's pay in advance."

Mr. Vivian took from his pocket-book a ten-dollar bill and placed it in Gilbert's hands.

"Under the circumstances," he said, "you may as well give up selling papers."

"I shall be very glad to give it up, sir, and now I shall feel able to do so."

"I appreciate and respect your motives in doing what you could find to do, but now you are a teacher,—a classical professor,—and must do nothing incompatible with the dignity of your learned profession."

"I will try to remember it, sir."

"I must leave you now. Let us see you this evening."

"I will be sure to come, sir."

When Gilbert left the hotel, he felt elated at his unexpected good fortune.

"I believe the tide has turned," he said to himself. "I little dreamed that my Latin would prove such a friend in need. I can't expect to earn the liberal sum Mr. Vivian has agreed to pay me, but I will do my duty as faithfully and well as I can."

Just after dinner that evening Alphonso Jones strolled into Gilbert's room.

"How is the newspaper business?" he inquired.

"Pretty fair," answered Gilbert.

"I think we ought to patronize Mr. Greyson, eh, Mr. Ingalls?"

"Thank you, Mr. Jones, but I have retired from the business."

"You don't say! Why, you told me it was fair."

"I shall retire nevertheless."

"Have you found another place?"

"I have obtained another position."

"You have! What is it?"

"Professor of the Classics and English Literature."

"You're joking," remarked Alphonso, rather bewildered.

"No, I am not. I have been engaged to teach five evenings in the week."

"I didn't know you were such a scholar," said Mr. Jones, surprised. "Do they pay you much?"

"Two dollars an evening."

"Good gracious! That is splendid pay."

"Yes, it is very good pay."

"Where are you to teach?"

"Mr. Vivian's son."

"He don't know that you have been a newsboy, does he?"

"Yes, he does; he saw me selling papers in the street to-day."

"Well, Greyson, all I can say is, you are the luckiest boy I ever knew. I wish I could earn two dollars an evening."

"I'll try to get you a chance," said Gilbert, demurely. "What can you teach?"

"Well, I aint very fresh in my studies," said Alphonso. "I guess it wouldn't be of any use. Aint you going to work in the daytime?"

"I shall get back into the broker's office if I can."

"Then you will have quite an income for a boy, Gilbert," said Mr. Ingalls.

"Don't you think you could take me up and introduce me to the Vivians some evening?" insinuated Alphonso.

"I don't think I could, Mr. Jones."

"Oh! it's of no consequence," said Alphonso, with apparent indifference. "I have any quantity of high-toned friends who move in the first circles. Some of them know the Vivians, and that's why I wanted to be introduced."

"I wonder if that fellow expects to be believed," said Mr. Ingalls, after Alphonso had retired.

CHAPTER XXXIII.

THE NEW PROFESSOR.

FRED VIVIAN had not been informed of the plan which his father had in view for him. Mr. Vivian, however, felt confident that it would be agreeable to his son, and did not wish to speak of it until he had ascertained Gilbert's willingness.

At dinner, after the interview described in the last chapter, Mr. Vivian for the first time mentioned the matter.

"What lessons have you to-night, Fred?" he asked.

"I have my Latin, and some hard sums in Reduction."

"How are you getting on in Latin?"

"I wish you would let me give it up, father," said Fred, earnestly. "I believe it was only got up to trouble school-boys."

"I suppose," said his father, smiling, "you think Cæsar, Virgil, and Cicero only wrote with the same purpose."

"Confound them! Why couldn't they write in English?" said Fred, petulantly.

All at the table laughed, and finally Fred himself joined in.

"I suspect the Roman boys would have found as much trouble with English as you find with Latin," said Mr. Vivian. "As a fact, there was no such language in existence then as our modern English tongue."

"I wish Latin were as easy as English," said Fred.

"No doubt it is. Foreigners find our language very difficult."

"Difficult! I don't see what there is difficult about it."

"Because it is your native language. Roman boys would have been equally surprised at any one finding Latin difficult."

"I wish I was a Roman boy, then. Laura, will you help me about my sums?"

"I have got my own lessons to prepare, Fred."

"Will you help me, father?"

"I like to have my evenings to myself, Fred. However, don't look disappointed. You shall have help."

"Who will help me? Laura says she can't."

"I have engaged a professor to come here every evening, and assist you about your lessons."

"A professor!" exclaimed Fred, uneasily. "That will be as bad as being at an evening school. I would rather get along by myself."

"Just now you wanted help," said his father.

"I don't want a professor. He will make me work too hard."

"I think you will like him," said Mr. Vivian.

"When is he coming?"

"This evening. He will be here about eight o'clock."

"Isn't this a new plan?" asked Mrs. Vivian.

"Don't you approve of it, my dear?" asked her husband.

"I thought his presence might be a restraint upon us, unless, indeed, Fred goes upstairs with him."

"No, let me stay here," urged Fred. "I don't want to go off with that old man."

"How do you know he is an old man?" inquired his father, smiling.

"I suppose he is."

"He can't be considered so. In fact, he is rather young."

"It's all the same," said Fred, discontentedly. "I suppose he is as stiff as a poker."

"He did not impress me so. With his help you will get through your lessons quickly; and then you can have the rest of the evening to yourself."

"What is his name?" asked Laura.

"I will see if I can find his card," said Mr. Vivian, pretending to search his pockets in vain. "Never mind, I will ask him when he comes."

"You did not tell me you thought of making this arrangement for Fred," said Mrs. Vivian.

"I see," said her husband, smiling, "that you are a little in doubt as to its expediency. If at the end of a week it appears unsatisfactory I will dismiss the professor."

Fred was relieved by this promise. He had already formed in his own mind an image of the expected teacher,—a tall, thin man, in a rusty-black suit, wearing a pair of iron-bowed spectacles. He had seen the tutor of a schoolmate of his who answered this description, and hastily adopted the conclusion that most visiting tutors were like him.

At ten minutes of eight Gilbert Greyson was announced.

"O Gilbert, I'm so glad to see you," said Fred; "though I'm afraid I can't be with you much this evening."

"Why not?" asked Gilbert.

"Father has engaged a professor to assist me in my studies; when you came in I thought at first it was he."

Gilbert read the joke in Mr. Vivian's smiling face, and determined to keep it up.

"What sort of a teacher is he?" he asked.

"I don't know. I suppose he's an old fogy in spectacles."

"Don't you think you shall like him?"

"Father says if I don't he'll send him off at the end of the week."

Again Gilbert smiled, and Mr. Vivian laughed outright.

"I don't see what you two are laughing about," said Fred.

"It's a good joke, Gilbert, isn't it?" said the merchant.

"Yes, sir."

"I don't see any joke," said Fred.

"Nor I," said Laura.

"Perhaps the professor may be willing to help you, if you require it, Laura," suggested her father.

"If he is such a man as Fred expects," said Laura, "I would rather get along by myself."

"It is hardly fair to take a prejudice against a person before you see him, Laura."

"I won't."

"For my own part, I was favorably impressed by what I saw of him."

"What does he look like? Is he tall?"

"No."

"Is he old?"

"No; quite young."

"Has he whiskers?"

"I didn't see any."

"Is he good-looking?"

"That is rather a delicate question, eh, Gilbert?"

"Yes, sir. I will answer it for you. He is not."

"What—do you know him, Gilbert?" asked Fred.

"He ought to," said Mr. Vivian. "He has seen him in his looking-glass every morning for sixteen years. There, the secret is out Fred, let me formally introduce you to Professor Gilbert,—the teacher I have engaged for you."

"Are you really to be my teacher, Gilbert?" asked Fred, delighted.

"If you conclude to keep me," said our hero, "you may decide to send me adrift at the end of the week."

GILBERT IN A NEW ROLE.

"I said that when I thought it was somebody else," said Fred. "Do you think you can show me how to do sums in Reduction?"

"I think I can," said Gilbert, smiling.

"I will get you to help me in Interest, Gilbert," said Laura.

"I thought you didn't want any help from your brother's teacher," said Mr. Vivian.

"I didn't know who it was to be then, papa. I'm glad you have engaged Gilbert."

"There is one more objection to you, Gilbert," said Mr. Vivian, seriously; "my wife thinks your presence may be a restraint upon us. She thinks you had better retire with Fred to some other part of the house."

"You have got the joke upon me too," said Mrs. Vivian. "I, too, was quite in the dark as to whom you had engaged. We don't look upon Gilbert in the light of a stranger, but rather as one of the family."

"Thank you, Mrs. Vivian," said our hero, gratefully.

"Then it appears, Gilbert, that you will be allowed to practise your vocation here. I would suggest that a pair of spectacles would make your appearance more impressive and dignified."

"I like you best as you are, Gilbert," said Fred, putting his arm around the neck of his new tutor.

"And I too," said Laura.

"Then I won't go to the expense of spectacles," said Gilbert. "Shall we begin now, Fred?"

Fred brought his arithmetic and slate, and Gilbert explained the sums in a familiar manner, making Fred do them himself.

"I understand them first-rate now," said Fred, in a tone of satisfaction. "You're a bully teacher, Gilbert."

"Now, shall we take the Latin?" asked Gilbert. "I'll try to be a *bully* teacher in that also."

By nine o'clock Fred's task was completed, and Gilbert transferred his attention to Laura. Fifteen minutes were all she required. The evening work being over, Gilbert played at games with his two pupils till ten, then rose to go.

"I'm so glad you're my teacher," said Fred. "Be sure to come to-morrow night."

"I am afraid you will get tired of me after a while, and want to discharge me," said Gilbert, smiling.

"Will you promise to stay with us till you are discharged?"

"Yes, Fred."

"Then it's all right," said Fred, in a tone of satisfaction.

Mr. Vivian found that he had done a very popular thing in engaging Gilbert, and was, in consequence, pleased himself.

"Well, Gilbert," said his room-mate, on his return, "how did your first lesson come off?"

"With flattering success. I never earned money more pleasantly in my life. My old teacher would stare if he should learn that I had set myself up as a classical professor."

"Your fortune has changed wonderfully. From a newsboy to professor is rather a startling transformation."

"My career as a newsboy is ended. I abandon the field to my competitors, and devote myself to the dissemination of learning."

"Alphonso Jones thinks you are a very remarkable young man. He told me so to-night."

"I can return the compliment," said Gilbert, laughing. "If you can change a ten-dollar bill, Mr. Ingalls, I will pay you the six dollars advanced for my board."

"You needn't be in a hurry, Gilbert."

"I don't like to be in debt. I can sleep better when I have paid up the loan."

"I shall be glad to lend you again if you need it."

"Thank you, Mr. Ingalls; but I hope I shan't need it."

Early the next morning Mr. Sands reached New York, having come through by night from Washington.

CHAPTER XXXIV.

THE BROKER'S RETURN.

ABOUT ten o'clock, on the morning of his arrival, Mr. Sands entered his office. He had kept the run of the business through letters from Mr. Moore, the book-keeper; but the latter had omitted to mention Gilbert's dismissal, and the reinstatement of John as his successor.

Mr. Sands was therefore surprised to see John in the office, with his hat off.

"Where is Gilbert?" he asked, abruptly.

John looked confused.

"He'll tell you," he said, pointing to his cousin.

"Have you dismissed Gilbert, Mr. Moore?" demanded Mr. Sands, abruptly.

Moore, in spite of his bravado, was a little nervous. He was apprehensive that he would not be able to convince Mr. Sands of Gilbert's guilt.

"I was obliged to discharge him, I am sorry to say," he answered.

"Why did you discharge him, may I inquire?" persisted the broker.

Simon Moore, himself of a haughty disposition, flushed at the imperative tone which his employer used. It chafed him especially to be so addressed in the presence of his young cousin.

"I don't suppose you wish to have a thief in your employ," he answered, hastily.

"Do you charge Gilbert Greyson with being a thief?"

"I do, sir."

"Let me know the particulars."

Simon Moore rehearsed the story, already familiar to the reader, of the ten-dollar bill found in the pocket of Gilbert's overcoat.

"Did he admit his guilt?" asked the broker.

"Oh, no, he brazened it out; but the proofs were overwhelming."

"Who found the bill in Gilbert's pocket?"

"John."

"Oh!" ejaculated the broker, significantly.

Simon Moore's face flushed again.

"Let me explain," he said.

"By all means; that is what I want."

"Only John, who had come in to make a call on me, and Gilbert had been here. One or the other must have been the thief. I therefore asked Gilbert to search John, and John to search Gilbert. It seemed to me fair. The result showed who was the thief."

"Upon this, you discharged Gilbert, and engaged John."

"Yes, sir. I needed a boy, and did not dare to employ Gilbert lest there should be further and more serious losses. John being present, and understanding the duties, I engaged him."

"John is your cousin, is he not, Mr. Moore?" asked Mr. Sands, quietly.

"Yes, sir," said the book-keeper, looking slightly embarrassed.

"It was very fortunate for him that he happened to be at the office on that particular morning."

Here John thought it time to introduce himself into the conversation.

"That's what Cousin Simon told me," he said.

"If John had not been here, I should have been obliged to advertise for a boy," said the book-keeper, recovering his confidence.

"Have you seen Gilbert since?" inquired Mr. Sands.

"I have," said John, grinning.

"Where did you see him? Do you know if he has another situation?"

"Oh, yes," said John, chuckling; "he's set up on his own account."

"What do you mean?"

"T'other morning I saw him selling papers near the City Hall Park."

"Humph!"

Mr. Sands said no more, but set about examining the books. Presently he put on his hat and went out.

"What do you think he's going to do, Cousin Simon?" asked John, anxiously.

"I guess the storm's blown over."

"He didn't seem to like it that I was here."

"He don't have a very high opinion of you; and I don't blame him," said the book-keeper, unable to restrain his sarcasm, although John was his cousin.

"Seems to me you're pretty hard on me," said John, aggrieved. "Do you think he'll let me stay?"

"I think he will, if you do your duty."

"Oh, I'll do that fast enough," said John, looking relieved.

"I advise you not to let Mr. Sands see you with a cigarette in your mouth."

"Who told you I smoked cigarettes? It's a—"

"You'd better not finish the sentence. I saw you last evening on the street with one in your mouth."

"I guess I'll have to be more careful," said John to himself. "Who'd have thought he'd find out?"

"I was just trying it to see how it seemed," he explained.

"Well, you know now, and you'd better give them up," said Simon Moore. "Now, go to the post-office for the mail."

On his way home, in the afternoon, Mr. Sands was looking about for a seat in the crowded car, when a boy addressed him.

"Take my seat, Mr. Sands."

"Gilbert!" exclaimed the broker, cordially, extending his hand. "I have been hoping to meet you."

"When did you get home from Washington, sir?"

"This morning early. I was surprised not to find you in your accustomed place in my office."

"I suppose Mr. Moore explained my absence?" said Gilbert.

"Yes; but I should prefer to hear your explanation. I should have more faith in its truth."

"Thank you, sir," said Gilbert, gratefully.

"It is hardly a matter to talk about in public. Have you any engagement this afternoon?"

"No, sir."

"Then come around to my house, and take dinner."

"What will Mr. Moore say?" asked Gilbert smiling.

"We will see to-morrow. Will you come?"

"With great pleasure, Mr. Sands."

Mr. Sands lived in a pleasant house up-town. He had a wife but no children. His wife greeted Gilbert pleasantly.

"I have heard my husband speak of you," she said.

Before dinner Gilbert got a chance to explain matters to Mr. Sands.

"I believe you," said the broker, emphatically.

"Don't rely too much upon my word, sir," said Gilbert. "I want you to be thoroughly convinced of my innocence."

"I am."

"Still, sir, I should like to bring a street boy—a boot-black—to confirm my story. He saw John put the bill into my overcoat pocket, when I was out on an errand."

"That is important testimony. I trust your word implicitly; but it may be as well to bring him round to the office, in order to confound those who have got up this wicked plot against you."

"He is only a boot-black," said Gilbert; "but I think he is trustworthy."

"I have reasons with which you are not acquainted for believing him and you," said the broker.

Gilbert looked curious, and Mr. Sands explained.

"I was present in an oyster-saloon, one evening before I started for Washington, and overheard Mr. Moore and John expressing their intentions to get you into trouble during my absence. This was the reason why I warned you against the book-keeper."

"I remember it, sir; but I did not know your reasons."

"Now, tell me how you have got along, being suddenly deprived of your income. John told me he saw you selling papers near City Hall Park one day."

"It is true, sir. I could make something that way, and so I tried it."

"I respect you the more for it. Have you kept up this employment till now?"

"No, sir. Mr. Vivian has engaged me as tutor for his son, at a salary of ten dollars per week."

"Is it possible? That is remarkable, considering your youth."

"It was to help me, sir, I have no doubt."

"You must be a good scholar."

"Not necessarily; Fred is only just beginning Latin, and it does not require much learning to teach him."

"If your time is so profitably occupied, I suppose I can't induce you to come back into my office."

"I should be very glad to do so, sir. I only give my evenings to Fred Vivian."

"Then you may come back to-morrow, at a salary of seven dollars a week."

"You are very kind, sir. I fear I shall not earn so much."

"That is my lookout. Come to-morrow, at quarter-past nine. If I am not there, say nothing to Mr. Moore about resuming your situation."

"All right, sir."

After dinner Gilbert went to Mr. Vivian's, to meet his pupil.

CHAPTER XXXV.

GILBERT'S TRIUMPH.

SHORTLY after the office opened on the following day, Simon Moore and John were disagreeably surprised by the entrance of Gilbert. He had found his witness, Tom, the boot-black, and requested him to remain outside, within call.

"What do you want here?" demanded the book-keeper, frowning.

"Has Mr. Sands returned?" asked our hero.

"No, he hasn't," replied Moore, with unblushing falsehood.

"I think you must be mistaken," said Gilbert, composedly; "for I saw him getting on a street-car yesterday."

"Then if you knew he was at home, why did you ask me?"

Gilbert did not think it necessary to answer this question.

"I will stop and speak to him," he said.

"No, you won't," said Simon Moore, roughly. "I know what you want. You want to make him believe you are innocent."

"You are right, Mr. Moore. I do wish to convince him of my innocence."

"I guess you've got cheek," put in John. "Didn't I find the money that was lost, in your overcoat pocket?"

"Yes."

"That's enough, I should say," said the book-keeper, dexterously availing himself of this admission. "You are a witness, John, that he has confessed the theft."

"If you twist what I say in that way," said Gilbert, indignantly, "there is no use in my saying anything."

"That is true enough. There is no use in your saying anything. Now, I've got something more to say. You've no business in this office; and the sooner you clear out the better."

"Yes, the sooner you clear out the better," chimed in John. "You've come here to get away my place; but you'd better give up trying. Mr. Sands is not such a fool as to believe you."

"Are you going?" demanded the book-keeper, menacingly. "John, put him out."

John advanced cautiously towards our hero, who smiled unterrified.

"Come, go out!—do you hear?" he said.

"I won't put you to the trouble of putting me out," said Gilbert, good-naturedly. "I'll step out for the present."

"And go away from here,—do you hear? Don't you hang around the office."

Gilbert, however, did not see fit to obey this last order. He waited in the neighborhood for Mr. Sands to arrive.

"He means to make trouble, Cousin Simon," said John, uneasily.

"He would like to, no doubt," responded the book-keeper; "but it would be very strange if Mr. Sands believed him against us."

"Well, I hope it'll all turn out right," said John; "but he's got a lot of cheek—that boy has. I wish you'd had him locked up."

"It might have been the best plan; but I think we can carry things through. Don't you put in your oar, or you may spoil the whole thing. Leave it to me."

"All right, Cousin Simon."

At the corner of Wall and New Streets Gilbert met Mr. Sands, who had come down-town, in a Broadway stage.

"I see you are on hand," said the broker. "Have you been to the office?"

"Yes, sir."

"What sort of a reception did you get from Mr. Moore?"

"He ordered me out."

The broker smiled.

"Perhaps it may be my turn to order out," he said. "Come back with me."

"Thank you, sir."

Simon Moore was not over-pleased when he saw Gilbert entering the office with his employer, but he said nothing. He waited to see how the land lay.

"Mr. Moore," said the broker, "I met Gilbert outside, and have brought him in to talk over the charge which you bring against him."

"He has been here already," said Moore, coldly, "and I ordered him out."

"It appears to me that this is rather summary treatment."

"I think I have treated him very indulgently. I might have had him arrested for theft, but I didn't want to be too hard upon him."

"You seem to take it for granted that he is guilty."

"He *must* be. He will himself admit that the missing bill was found in his overcoat pocket; ask him, if you like, sir."

Mr. Sands turned to Gilbert.

"It is true," he said.

"That is all that need be said," said the book-keeper, shrugging his shoulders.

"It does not necessarily follow that he put the bill in himself," remarked Mr. Sands.

"Who else could have done it?" demanded Moore, triumphantly.

"I will answer that question," said Gilbert. "John put the money in my pocket, in order to get me into a scrape."

"Do you hear that, Cousin Simon?" exclaimed John, with virtuous indignation. "I didn't think Gilbert could be so wicked as to say such things."

"I expected it," said Moore, regarding Gilbert maliciously. "A boy that will steal will lie also. Of course he only says it to screen himself."

Gilbert listened to this outbreak very composedly. He knew that his employer was on his side, and did not think it necessary to contradict it.

"Have you any proof of your statement, Gilbert?" asked Mr. Sands.

"Of course he hasn't," said Moore, contemptuously. "It rests upon his word; and that is worth nothing. Ask him if he saw John put the money in his pocket."

"No, I did not," answered Gilbert, without waiting for Mr. Sands to put the question.

"I thought not," said Moore, triumphantly. "You only suspected it."

"Somebody saw it done," said Gilbert. "Shall I call him?"

The question was addressed to Mr. Sands, who nodded his head.

Gilbert went to the door, and called Tom.

Tom, the boot-black, shuffled in, with his box strapped to his back.

"Tom," said Gilbert, "did you, one day, see John—that boy there—putting a bill in my coat-pocket?"

"Yes," answered Tom, "shure I did; but I thought it was his own, and it was no harm, till you told me how you'd lost your place."

Mr. Sands put two or three questions, which Tom answered in a straightforward manner. Then he turned to the book-keeper.

"What do you say to this, Mr. Moore?" he asked.

"I say that it is all a lie," returned the book-keeper, angrily. "How much are you paid for lying?" he demanded, sharply, of the boot-black.

"Not a cent," said Tom, indignantly; "and it isn't a lie either, you spalpeen! You knew all about it, too. I saw you lookin' at him when he did it."

"I'd like to thrash you, within an inch of your life, you impudent young blackguard!" said Simon Moore, furiously.

"You'd better not try it," said Tom, boldly.

"I hope, Mr. Sands," said Moore, turning to the broker, "that you are not going to believe this young ragamuffin against me. It is a pretty state of things, if my word is to be disputed by such as he."

"Mr. Moore," said the broker, gravely, "I regret to say that, in this instance, I am forced to believe him rather than you. Wait a moment,"—seeing that Moore was going to interrupt him,—"it is only fair that I should give you my reason. Possibly you will remember one evening when, at an oyster-saloon, you and John concerted this very plot against Gilbert. I was in the next stall, and overheard all you both said. I was not, therefore, surprised to learn, upon my return, under what circumstances Gilbert had been discharged."

Simon Moore and John looked at each other in silent dismay. Both remembered well the conversation alluded to.

"If I am the object of such suspicion," blustered Moore, at length, "I don't think I had better remain in your employ."

"I approve your decision," said the broker, gravely.

"I will leave at once, if you say so."

Just then a young man entered the office.

"You are at liberty to do so," said Mr. Sands. "I have already engaged this gentleman as your successor."

"I guess I'll go, too," said John.

"You may. Gilbert, you will resume your old place."

It would be difficult to paint the anger and mortification upon the faces of the two cousins as they left the office.

"This comes from trying to help you, you young loafer," said Moore, savagely, turning upon John. "But for you I should have kept my place."

"I'm sure I aint to blame," said John, whining.

"You are wholly to blame. I shall thrash you some day."

John thought this rather hard, since the plot was of his cousin's contriving. I may remark here that months passed before Simon Moore obtained another situation.

CHAPTER XXXVI.

MR. BRIGGS RETURNS FROM EUROPE.

SO Gilbert was reinstated in his old position, at an advanced salary. His income was now seventeen dollars a week,—an amount which enabled him to live very comfortably, and even to lay aside a few dollars every week. Of course, this required the exercise of economy; but Gilbert felt it to be his duty to be prudent, and prepare for a time when his income might be less.

He found the new book-keeper a very different man from Mr. Moore. He was quite as efficient, and far more agreeable. From the first he regarded Gilbert with friendly interest, and treated him as a friend.

For some time Gilbert had seen nothing of Randolph Briggs. The latter occasionally condescended to wonder how that beggar Greyson was getting along, but did not feel any very deep anxiety on his account. One day, however, Randolph ventured down-town, and had the curiosity to enter Mr. Sands' office.

The book-keeper chanced to be out, and Gilbert was in charge.

Randolph stared in astonishment at our hero.

"How do you happen to be here?" he asked, abruptly.

"Why shouldn't I be here?" returned Gilbert, pleasantly. "This is my place of business."

"But, I say, I thought you were sent off."

"So I was."

"How did you get back?"

"Mr. Sands took me back, and discharged the book-keeper."

"Whew!" exclaimed Randolph. "He must think a good deal of you."

"He believed the charge to be false, and that it was a conspiracy against me."

Randolph did not know what to think. He had predicted that Gilbert would never get back; and it is not pleasant to be mistaken in one's predictions.

"Do you board at the same place?" he asked, after a while.

"Yes."

"Don't you find it hard to pay your board?"

Gilbert smiled. The question was an impertinent one; but he felt amused rather than offended.

"I have paid regularly so far," he said.

"How did you do when you were out of a place?"

"I lived on my salary as teacher."

Randolph opened wide his eyes in astonishment.

"What do you mean?" he asked.

"I teach in the evening," explained our hero.

"You don't say so! Why, you are only a boy!"

"But I know enough to teach a younger boy."

"Who are you teaching?"

"Fred Vivian."

"What, Laura's brother?"

"The same."

"He don't come to your room, does he?"

"No, I go there five evenings in the week."

"Do you get much pay?"

"I don't think you can expect me to answer that question, Randolph."

"Why, aint you willing to tell?"

"I'll tell you so much,—that Mr. Vivian pays me more than Mr. Sands."

Randolph was silent for a moment. This news was worse than the other. He had an admiration for Laura, and it was very disagreeable to think that while he was not on visiting terms at her house, this boy, so much his social inferior, should be freely admitted to Laura's presence. Perhaps, however, he only saw Fred.

"Does Laura come into the room when you teach her brother?" he asked.

"Certainly. In fact, I help her a little too."

"It's the strangest thing I ever heard of," muttered Randolph.

"What is?"

"That Mr. Vivian should take a poor office-boy to teach his children."

"It is strange, but true," assented Gilbert, smiling.

"I didn't think you were so artful."

"What do you mean?"

"If you hadn't been artful, you wouldn't have got so thick with the Vivians."

"I don't want to get angry with you, Randolph, but I don't like that remark. Suppose we change the subject. What do you hear from your father?"

"He was in Manchester when we last heard from him."

"When do you expect him home?"

"In a month or six weeks."

"You must be glad to have him return."

"Oh, I don't know," said Randolph. "I'm having a pretty good time."

"He don't seem to have overmuch affection for his father," thought Gilbert. And Gilbert was right. Randolph was very selfish; and his chief regard was for himself. Even his mother, who idolized him, received but a scant return. One reason why Randolph would be sorry to have his father return was, that he was now receiving, from his mother, the six dollars a week which properly should have gone for Gilbert's board; and of this he would doubtlessly be deprived when Mr. Briggs came back.

"Well, I guess I can't stay any longer," said Randolph, looking at his watch. "You haven't been up to the house lately."

"No; my evenings are engaged, you know."

"You'd better come up and dine soon."

Gilbert was rather surprised at this invitation; but Randolph's motive was soon apparent.

"If you will, I will go round to the Vivians afterwards with you."

"Perhaps," suggested Gilbert, "when I want to be away for an evening, you will go in my place."

"No, I guess not. I don't think I should like to teach. I'd rather go with you."

"I will think of it. At any rate, I thank you for the invitation."

Randolph went home at once. He wanted to tell his mother the news. It may well be believed that she was not pleased. She would have been glad to hear that he had been compelled to leave the city.

"It seems," said she, sharply, "that Mr. Briggs is not the only fool in the city."

"I wonder what father would say to hear that," chuckled Randolph.

"You know what I mean. He was perfectly infatuated with that Greyson boy; and now it appears that Mr. Vivian is just as much of a dupe."

"He's very artful," suggested Randolph.

"That is the very word to use," said Mrs. Briggs, energetically. "It does credit to your insight into character."

"I always thought he was artful," said Randolph, much flattered.

"He never deceived *me*," said his mother, emphatically. "I felt instinctively that he was a boy to be shunned. I dare say he would like to ingratiate himself with your father so far as to induce him to adopt him, and put him on an equality with you."

"By gracious, I hope not," exclaimed Randolph, alarmed.

"He shall never do it with my consent," said Mrs. Briggs, energetically. "Fortunately you have a mother, who is devoted to you, my son."

"Of course you are, mother. You won't let father pay Gilbert's board, after he gets back will you?"

"Not if I can help it."

"And you'll persuade him to give the extra amount to me?"

"I will do my best; but your father is sometimes very obstinate."

"It takes you to manage him, mother. Just let him know what you think of Gilbert."

"He knows that very well already; but I will do my best for you, Randolph."

Six weeks later Mr. Briggs arrived in New York. Gilbert saw his name in a list of the passengers by the last Cunard steamer, but decided not to call upon him immediately.

"He would think I was applying to have my board paid again," he said to himself; "and that is no longer necessary."

CHAPTER XXXVII.

AN IMPORTANT REVELATION.

GILBERT did not lose sight of the little flower-girl whom he had befriended. Even when his fortunes were at the lowest, he never failed to buy a bouquet of her daily. More than this he did not feel able to do then. But as soon as he obtained the position of Fred's teacher, he again visited Mr. Talbot in his poor lodgings, and gave him more substantial assistance. The sick man improved steadily in health and spirits. It did him great good to feel that he had a friend, though that friend was only a boy, dependent on his earnings for support.

On the day after he had heard of Mr. Briggs' return from Europe, Gilbert made a hurried call during his dinner-hour.

"How are you to-day, Mr. Talbot?" he asked.

"I am better," said the sick man. "I hope I shall soon be well enough to go to work again."

"I think you will," said Gilbert, cheerfully. "I must try to see what I can find for you to do, among my business friends."

"Thank you; do you know many business men?"

"No," answered Gilbert. "I wonder," he said, half to himself, "whether my guardian couldn't give you work."

"Your guardian!" repeated Mr. Talbot, in surprise.

"Yes," said Gilbert, smiling; "but you mustn't think because I have a guardian that I have any property."

"Who is your guardian?"

"Mr. Richard Briggs, a New York merchant. He only got home from Europe yesterday."

"Richard Briggs!" exclaimed the sick man in evident excitement.

"Yes; do you know anything of him?"

"His name is very familiar to me. Tell me, are you the son of James Greyson, formerly a merchant in the West Indies?"

It was Gilbert's turn to be excited.

"My father died in the West Indies," he answered; "but I know very little of him. Did you know him, Mr. Talbot?"

"I ought to know him. I was his book-keeper up to the time of his death."

"Is it possible?" ejaculated Gilbert. "How glad I am to meet you! I know nothing of my father except what Mr. Briggs has told me."

"One thing I do not understand," continued the sick man. "You say you have no property; but this cannot be. Your father left seventy-five thousand dollars."

"Seventy-five thousand dollars! Are you sure, Mr. Talbot?"

"No one can be surer. I knew all about your father's business and the extent of his property."

"Was this money entrusted to my guardian?" asked Gilbert, quickly.

"It was. Your father and Richard Briggs were schoolmates, so I have heard him say; and he felt sufficient confidence in him to confide you to his care."

It is not a pleasant moment when for the first time we are led to suspect those in whom we have confided; and important and welcome as the intelligence otherwise was, Gilbert felt sober at the treachery of Mr. Briggs. The latter, as we have seen, had been kinder to him than his wife or son, and Gilbert had felt grateful. Even now he could not rid himself of a certain feeling of kindness to his guardian, false as he had been to his trust.

"I am sorry to hear this," he said, gravely.

"Sorry to hear that your father left you a fortune?"

"I don't mean that. I am sorry that my guardian has been wicked enough to attempt to cheat me out of it."

"What sort of a man is Mr. Briggs?"

"At first I was not prepossessed in his favor; but he improved on acquaintance. When his wife and son spoke against me, he always took my part. When I was charged with dishonesty, he refused to believe it."

"I think it quite possible that he is a naturally kind-hearted man," said the sick man; "but human nature is sometimes inconsistent. I think it may have been in a moment of embarrassment that he appropriated your fortune. If he has since prospered, it may be possible for you to recover it."

"Are you sure it was as much as seventy-five thousand dollars, Mr. Talbot?" asked Gilbert, dazzled as he well might be by the magnitude of the sum.

"I am sure of it."

"Can you prove it, so that Mr. Briggs will be compelled to give it up to me?"

"Fortunately I can. I have in my trunk a document, in your father's own handwriting, giving a schedule of his property, in which he expressly says that he makes it over in trust to Richard Briggs, for your use. Indeed, it must now amount to more than seventy-five thousand dollars; for only a small part of the income has been expended for you. Probably a few hundreds of dollars a year are all that have been spent for you."

"I don't see how Mr. Briggs could make such false representations," said Gilbert, thoughtfully.

"'Money is the root of all evil,' my young friend. It is an old proverb, and unfortunately a true one."

"I have noticed one thing," continued our hero. "When I thanked Mr. Briggs for paying my board, as I supposed, out of his own pocket, he always seemed uncomfortable and embarrassed."

"That shows he is not wholly without shame."

"It is about time for me to be going back to the office, Mr. Talbot; but before I go I want to ask your advice on one point. How soon shall I speak to Mr. Briggs on this subject?"

"Whenever you have an opportunity."

"Of course, I must refer to you as my informant."

"By all means," said the sick man, promptly. "It will be a great satisfaction to me if, through my means, you succeed in obtaining your rights."

For the rest of the day and through the evening Gilbert's mind was occupied with the important intelligence he had learned. He did not make a confidant of any one, feeling that it was not yet time.

Mr. Ingalls, his room-mate, saw that he was thinking busily about something, but did not make any inquiries. He knew that Gilbert would let him know when he got ready. Alphonso Jones was not so forbearing.

"By Jove! Greyson, I believe you are in love," he said, abruptly.

"What makes you think so, Mr. Jones?"

"You've been sitting with your eyes fixed on the carpet for five minutes without speaking a word."

"Your opinion about love is worth something, Mr. Jones," said Gilbert, smiling. "You know how it is yourself. Didn't I see you walking with a fair widow last evening?"

"Who do you mean?" asked Alphonso, smiling.

"Mrs. Kinney, of course."

"I only happened to meet her going to a concert with Mr. Pond," exclaimed Alphonso. "He was called away a moment, and left her in my care."

"He was very imprudent," said Mr. Ingalls. "You know, Jones, you're a regular lady-killer. I really hope you won't try any of your fascinations on the widow."

Mr. Jones simpered, and was evidently pleased. It was his private opinion that he was unusually fascinating, and this public acknowledgment of it was gratifying.

"You will have your joke, Mr. Ingalls," he said. "I have a high respect for Mrs. Kinney; but, really, there is nothing in it, I do assure you."

"Time will show," said Mr. Ingalls, nodding his head in an oracular way. "But don't be precipitate, Mr. Jones. Remember the Countess de Montmorency, who may yet be your bride."

"I have no hopes in that quarter," said Alphonso, who had ascertained that the count had been reduced by family misfortunes to accept a position in a barbers shop. "Good-evening, gents."

When Alphonso had retired, Gilbert said, "I have something on my mind, Mr. Ingalls, though not what Mr. Jones supposed. I hope soon to let you know what it is."

"Whenever you are ready, Gilbert. I am not curious; but shall be interested in anything that concerns you. It isn't anything unpleasant, I hope."

"It may be greatly to my advantage."

"If that is the case, I can wait cheerfully."

CHAPTER XXXVIII.

GILBERT'S SHIP COMES IN.

IT may well be supposed that Gilbert wished, as soon as possible, to question his guardian on a subject having such an important bearing upon his future career. It occurred to him that it might be well to consult a lawyer first; but he finally decided not to do so. Personally Mr. Briggs had treated him kindly, and he did not wish, unless it should prove absolutely necessary, to assume a position antagonistic to him.

Gilbert reached his guardian's house about eight o'clock in the evening. He had received a note from Fred Vivian, stating that he was going to the theatre, and would not require a lesson that evening. This gave him abundant time for the interview.

Mrs. Briggs and Randolph had gone to make a call, and Gilbert found Mr. Briggs alone. In dressing-gown and slippers he was conning the evening paper when Gilbert was announced.

"Good-evening, Gilbert," said Mr. Briggs, cordially. "I am glad to see you."

"Thank you, sir," said Gilbert, gravely.

"I was feeling a little lonely. Mrs. Briggs and Randolph have gone out to make a call. How have you got on since I went away?"

"I am doing well now, sir; but at one time my prospects looked dark."

"How is that?" asked Mr. Briggs, surprised. "I thought I left you well provided for."

It was Gilbert's turn to look surprised.

"Didn't Randolph tell you about my losing my situation?" he asked.

"Not a word. How came you to lose it?"

Gilbert told the story, already familiar to the reader. He also told about his regaining it.

"That must have been disagreeable; and, of course, you felt the loss of income. But your board was at least provided for. You received money for that from my office?"

"No, sir; not a cent."

"Why not? I left directions to that effect."

Gilbert's cheek flushed.

"I called on Mrs. Briggs, to inquire about it," he said, reluctantly; "but she chose to treat me as a beggar, and I declined to receive anything."

Mr. Briggs looked annoyed.

"I am afraid," he said, desirous of excusing his wife, "that you are too sensitive, Gilbert. Mrs. Briggs is a little unfortunate in her manner, and gave you a wrong impression. However, you shall not suffer for it. Come round to the office to-morrow, and I will give you a sum equal to what you would have had if I had been at home."

"Thank you, sir," said Gilbert; but still he looked grave.

"Does not that satisfy you?" asked Mr. Briggs, a little annoyed.

Gilbert felt that the time had come for his question.

"I came here to-night, Mr. Briggs," he commenced, "to ask you a question."

"Ask it, of course," said the merchant, quite unprepared for what was coming.

Gilbert fixed his clear, penetrating eyes on his guardian's face.

"My father left you some money in trust for me; did he not, sir?"

"Certainly. I told you so."

"I know it, sir. Will you tell me what it amounted to?"

"Really," said Mr. Briggs, uncomfortably, "I can't tell without looking over my papers. What makes you ask?"

"Did it not amount to seventy-five thousand dollars?" demanded Gilbert, quietly.

Richard Briggs nearly started from his seat in surprise and dismay. That was the amount, as he well knew; but how on earth could the boy have found out? He saw that his ward had obtained some dangerously accurate information somewhere; and that he was thoroughly in earnest in his inquiry.

"Who could have put such a thought into your head?" he asked, slowly and hesitatingly.

"I won't make a secret of it," said Gilbert. "I have made the acquaintance of a man who knew my father. He tells me he was his book-keeper up to the time of his death. He claims to know all about my father's affairs, and the amount of property he left."

"There is some great mistake," muttered the merchant.

"I don't think there can be. Mr. Talbot has, in his possession, and has showed to me, an autograph-letter of my father, in which he gives full details on this subject."

"Where is this Talbot?" asked Mr. Briggs, abruptly.

"He is living in this city."

"Where?"

"You must excuse me, Mr. Briggs. At present I do not wish to tell you."

"He may be an impostor."

"I have thought of that; but such an imposition could not be carried out. I think he tells the truth."

"Suppose I believe the contrary,—what, then?"

"You have reason to know whether what he says is correct or not, Mr. Briggs," said Gilbert, resolutely. "If you deny it, and assert that he is an impostor, I will consult a lawyer, and have him cross-examine him on the subject, and give me his opinion."

"You have not spoken to a lawyer yet?" said Mr. Briggs, uneasily.

"No, sir."

"Lawyers are fond of instituting lawsuits. Probably one would report favorably."

"I should want to know his grounds. And I would not consent to a suit, unless he convinced me there was good ground for it."

"Gilbert," said the merchant, "I feel friendly to you, and I want you to succeed. Say no more about this affair, and to-morrow I will make over to you bank-shares amounting to ten thousand dollars. That will give you a good start in life."

"I only want what is my own," said Gilbert, sturdily. "I want what my father left me."

Mr. Briggs rose, and paced the room in silence. His good and bad angel were contending for the supremacy. The conflict came to an end, and his better nature triumphed. He resumed his seat, looking no longer perplexed or troubled, but as one who had thrown off a burden.

"Gilbert," he said, "it is all true. I have tried to be a villain; but I won't be one any longer. Your father left you a fortune, and it shall be restored to you."

Gilbert rose, and grasped Mr. Briggs' hand cordially. Boy as he was, he comprehended the struggle through which his guardian had passed.

"Thank you, sir," he said. "I shall forget all that has passed; and I ask you to remain my guardian, and take care of my property for me."

Man of the world as he was, Mr. Briggs was touched by this proof of generous confidence.

"I don't deserve this, Gilbert; but I will do as you ask. I will, however, see a lawyer, and make such arrangements that whatever may happen to me you will be safe."

At that moment the bell rang.

"I think Mrs. Briggs and Randolph have returned," said the merchant. "One word, Gilbert, of what has passed between us, let it only be known that you have received a large legacy, and that I am your guardian in reality as well as in name."

"All right, sir. Perhaps I had better go. Mrs. Briggs don't like me."

Her husband laughed.

"She will change when she knows you are rich," he said. "Don't be surprised. It is the way of the world."

He had scarcely finished when Mrs. Briggs entered, followed by Randolph. She remarked Gilbert's presence with displeasure.

"You here?" she said.

"Yes, my dear," said Mr. Briggs, pleasantly. "Gilbert has been keeping me company."

"He came *on business*, I suppose," sneered the lady.

"You are right, my dear. What made you guess his errand?"

"I supposed he wanted help," said Mrs. Briggs. "He wants his pension restored, of course."

"Is that what you came for, Gilbert?" asked Randolph, uncomfortably.

Gilbert rather enjoyed the misapprehension of his two enemies, but he left Mr. Briggs to answer.

"Really, my dear, you are hardly polite to my young ward."

"Your ward! Don't be ridiculous, Mr. Briggs. You know he hasn't got a cent, and has to live on charity."

"You are quite mistaken, my dear. Gilbert has just come into a property of over eighty thousand dollars. And he has asked me to take charge of it for him."

Mrs. Briggs sank into a chair in utter stupefaction, while Randolph opened his eyes in astonishment.

"You are jesting!" Mrs. Briggs managed to utter.

"Not at all. Is what I say correct, Gilbert?"

"I believe it is, sir."

It is singular how Gilbert was transformed all at once in the eyes of the worldly woman, and her son. Circumstances were changed, and they must change with them. It was awkward, but it must be done.

"I congratulate you, Gilbert," she said, trying to smile. "You are certainly very fortunate."

"I should say he was!" exclaimed Randolph. "I say, Gilbert, come and live with us, won't you?"

"I should really be glad to have my husband's ward in my family," said Mrs. Briggs, as graciously as possible.

"Thank you," said Gilbert; "but this has come upon me so suddenly, that I don't know what arrangements I shall make."

"Who left you this fortune?" asked Mrs. Briggs, curiously.

"We are not at liberty to go into particulars," said Mr. Briggs; "but there is no doubt about it."

"If you will excuse me, Mr. Briggs, I will leave you now. I should like to tell my friends of my good fortune."

"Certainly. Come to my counting-room in the morning at ten. Some arrangements will need to be made."

"I will be on hand, sir."

"Dine with us to-morrow, Gilbert," said Mrs. Briggs, graciously. "Randolph will be so glad of your company."

"Thank you."

Gilbert thought it due to his guardian to accept. He was wise enough to take the world as he found it, and return courtesy with courtesy.

"What has happened, Gilbert?" exclaimed his room-mate, when, half an hour later, Gilbert broke into the room, his face full of excitement.

"I am rich, Mr. Ingalls. I have become heir to eighty thousand dollars."

"Good gracious!" exclaimed Alphonso Jones, who was present. "I suppose you will go to live on Fifth Avenue among the swells."

"Not at present, Mr. Jones."

"I am very glad of your good luck, Gilbert," said his room-mate, warmly. "You must tell me all about it by and by."

"I wish I had eighty thousand dollars," said Alphonso. "Wouldn't I be high-toned?"

"Can't one be high-toned without being rich, Mr. Jones?" asked Gilbert.

Mr. Jones thought not; but he made one mental reservation. He privately thought himself high-toned, though he certainly was not rich.

CHAPTER XXXIX.

CONCLUSION.

NOWHERE did Gilbert receive heartier congratulations on the change in his fortunes than from Mr. Vivian and his family. Fred only was disturbed.

"I suppose you won't be willing to teach me any more, now you are rich, Gilbert," he said.

"I don't think it will make any difference, Fred," said Gilbert; "but I must consult your father about my plans."

"What are your own views and wishes, Gilbert?" asked the merchant.

"I want to get a better education," said Gilbert. "I should like to carry out my original plan, and go to college. After I graduate I may devote myself to business; but a good education won't interfere with that."

"I approve your plan," said Mr. Vivian. "Of course you will resign your place at the broker's."

"Yes, sir."

"Then I shall submit a plan for your future. We all like you, and you can be of use to Fred. Come and live with us. You can complete your preparation for college at some first-class school in the city, and enter next summer, if you like."

"I hope you will come, Gilbert," said Laura.

It might have been her voice which decided Gilbert to accept. At any rate, he did accept gratefully; and in less than a week he was installed at Mr. Vivian's as a member of the family.

Mr. Sands was sorry to lose his services, but acknowledged that it was better for him to give up his place. The day after his retirement he was sitting in Madison Park, when John, who had once caused him to lose his place, espied him. John had not yet succeeded in securing a place, nor had Mr. Moore, the book-keeper.

"What brings you here at this time in the day?" asked John, in surprise.

"I am a gentleman of leisure," answered Gilbert.

"Have you left Mr. Sands?" asked John, eagerly.

"Yes."

"Been bounced, eh?" asked John, radiantly.

Gilbert smiled. He understood John's feelings.

"No," he answered. "I left of my own accord."

"You haven't got another place?"

"No."

"Then it's too thin, your leaving of your own accord."

"It does look so, I admit," said Gilbert, good-humoredly. "But it is true, nevertheless."

"Why did you leave, then? You haven't had a fortune left you?"

"You've hit it, John. I no longer need my pay. I have become rich, and shall go on preparing for college."

"Is that really so?"

"It is quite true."

"Some folks are lucky," said John, enviously. "I aint one of that kind. I wish I could get your old place."

"I am afraid Mr. Sands wouldn't take you back. I wish he would, and that you would do so well that he would keep you."

"That will do to say; but you wouldn't help me back."

"Yes, I would, and will. I will go down to the office now, and ask Mr. Sands to take you back."

"You will, after the mean way I have treated you?" exclaimed John, in surprise.

"I don't bear any malice, John," said Gilbert. "Here, take my hand, and look upon me as a friend. If I can't get you back into my old place, I'll try elsewhere. Come, let us take the cars down-town, and I'll see what I can do for you."

"What a good fellow you are, Gilbert!" said John, much moved. "I am ashamed of trying to injure you."

"You didn't know me, then. But, John, will you try to give satisfaction, if you are taken back?"

"Yes, I will," said John, earnestly.

Half an hour later they entered the broker's office. No boy had been engaged as yet. Mr. Sands did not at first regard John's application with favor; though, as he understood the duties of the place, he could, if he pleased, do better than a new boy. Finally, the broker agreed to take him on trial.

"Remember, John," he said, "you owe your place to Gilbert's intercession. But for that I wouldn't take you back."

"I know it, sir. I hope you won't be sorry."

Here it may be said that John turned over a new leaf, and succeeded in this last trial in giving satisfaction. His cousin, Simon Moore, called him mean-spirited for going back; but John felt that he must look out for his own interests now, and did not regard his objection.

In his prosperity Gilbert did not forget Mr. Talbot and his little daughter. While he continued sick our hero allowed him a weekly sum sufficient to support father and daughter comfortably; and on his recovery he found him employment, and a more comfortable lodging. Little Emma was no longer obliged to go into the streets to sell bouquets, but was put at a good day-school. From time to time Gilbert called upon them, and was rejoiced to see the improved looks and happier faces of Emma and her father.

In the first chapter of this story the reader will recall John Munford, a school-friend of Gilbert, the son of a carpenter, who, on account of his father's poverty, was obliged to leave school, and go to work. Gilbert, in becoming rich, did not forget his early friend. One day John received a letter from Gilbert, in which, after speaking of his change of fortune, he wrote:—

"Now, John, I have a large income,—much more than I can use,—and I want to do what good I can with it. I know you want to keep at school, but cannot, on account of your father's circumstances. I have a proposal to make to you. Give up work, and go back to Dr. Burton's school. I will allow you three hundred dollars a year till you are ready to go to college. Then you shall come to Yale, and room with me. I will provide for you in college. After you graduate, your education will command a position that will make you independent. Let me know at once if you accept, or rather write me that you do accept."

What could John do, but to accept this generous offer with deep gratitude to his old school-fellow? Need it be said that Gilbert fulfilled his promise to the letter. Last year the two friends graduated, both taking high rank; and John is now principal of a High School in a Massachusetts town. Gilbert has decided to lead a business life, and has entered Mr. Vivian's establishment. He will be junior partner at the end of three years. He may form another partnership with a member of Mr. Vivian's family. I cannot say positively, but I think it quite probable.

Mr. Briggs is no longer Gilbert's guardian. Our hero is of age, and has assumed the charge of his own property. He is always sure of a cordial welcome from Mrs. Briggs now, and Randolph cultivates his intimacy; but Gilbert does not find him congenial. He is inclined to be dissipated, and, I am afraid, will not turn out well. But his mother upholds him on all occasions; and her ill-judged indulgence is partly the cause of her son's lack of promise.

Gilbert sometimes visits the old boarding-house. Mr. Ingalls is prospering. Alphonso Jones now boasts of his intimacy with Gilbert. It is rumored that he has offered himself to Mrs. Kinney, a young widow, already mentioned, and been rejected. His heart is not broken, however; and he is now a suitor for the hand of Miss Brintnall, the strong-minded school-teacher. She is "high-toned" in one sense, at least, as he will probably find after marriage.

The next volume of this series will be

WORK AND HOPE;

OR,

BEN BRADFORD'S MOTTO.

www.ingramcontent.com/pod-product-compliance
Lightning Source LLC
LaVergne TN
LVHW090518110826
845146LV00003B/905

* 9 7 8 9 3 5 7 9 4 2 0 6 5 *